FRIED CHICKEN & FRIENDS

THE HARTSYARD FAMILY COOKBOOK

GREGORY LLEWELLYN & NAOMI HART

THUNDER BAY
P·R·E·S·S
San Diego, California

CONTENTS

FOREWORD
HART TRANSPLANT

Oscar Wilde once famously noted, "Fashion is a form of ugliness so intolerable that we have to alter it every six months." And so it was that amid the slider and taco tsunami of 2012, an unassuming new restaurant opened on an unloved stretch of Enmore Road in Sydney's inner west.

The site had previously been endured for several years by a dour-faced purveyor of Nordic cuisine, whose initial mystification at why the kale and quinoa crowd weren't smitten by the prospect of whole-roasted piglet washed down by *glogg* had hardened to an embittered capitulation.

The space then reopened as Hartsyard, with the only hint at its menu being the words "seed and feed" on the sign outside. Before you even got a look at the menu, though, you were greeted by a ray of strawberry blonde sunshine in Naomi Hart, a front-of-house dynamo and ex-Broadway hoofer who'd returned to her homeland with an American hubby who reckoned he knew his way around a kitchen.

Managing a semi-subterranean work area of baseball-capped rogues and vagabonds was New Yorker Gregory Llewellyn. Although his Manhattan résumé was as expansive as it was impressive, Gregory instinctively knew he was only ever as good as his last plate.

Much like a musician who spends years finding his voice, Gregory had concocted a culinary Ramones with a nice schmear of Patsy Cline. His flavors were pure American ballsyness, the portions in generous contrast to the artsy disappearing-up-their-own rémoulade contrivances being served in the "hot" eateries across town.

Conjuring an equilibrium between the familiar and the challenging, the delicate and the robust, he created a menu that would garner accolades and acclaim from serious critics and one-upping bloggers eager to stake their claim as being the first to write up the Yard. The only thing missing was the pretension. In fact, you could check it in at the divey bar across the road, where you would routinely be despatched while your table was readied.

Do a shift in Gregory's kitchen and meet his sparkly eyed mother, Franny—two privileges this writer has had—and it quickly becomes apparent that generosity of spirit is paramount. Don't talk about what you're going to do, just shut up and get on with it. Praise is a dish for others to offer.

The item that exemplifies the Hartsyard phenomenon and the reason you're holding this book is the fried chicken. Crunchy, succulent, and tender—not to mention smothered in low-country sausage gravy—it is a moreish evocation of bold, honest rural Americana, with just a hint of trailer-park couldn't-give-a-continental. It is to be toasted with Lynyrd Skynyrd and Jack Daniel's. Which, like Naomi and Gregory, will always have a home in Australia.

DAVID SMIEDT
Hartsyard regular & friend

INTRODUCTION
GETTING ACROSS THE LINE

Gregory has been cooking since he was fifteen, when he skateboarded to the only restaurant close enough to his home in rural Johnson, in upstate New York. As a young adult, he dabbled briefly in snowboarding, but he soon realized he preferred the adrenaline of a bustling restaurant mid-service on a Saturday night, a rail full of tickets, and fifteen plates on the pass.

Me? I've been a nun, a cow, a duckling, a whore, a servant, a princess, and a dancing plate. That is to say, I used to perform in musical theater and we met when I was in New York City living the dream. Well, maybe not quite the dream. I was very happy, but from memory I was also very poor and pretty tired. But then we opened a restaurant just after we'd had a baby, and I quickly recalibrated my thoughts on poverty and fatigue.

It's not a particularly original tale. We met at a restaurant where I was the hostess and he was the chef. We dated in secret, and married eighteen months later at a converted foundry in Queens. I always knew he wanted his own restaurant, and I always said I'd help him open it. He does back of house and I do front. And so it follows with this book. He led the charge on the recipes and I filled in the rest. But there's the rub.

He likes fried chicken; I don't. He likes mashed potatoes; I like salad. He likes beer; I like dessert. It was just like the stage. Artistic differences already. So we decided to combine our likes and invite you all to one big Hartsyard fried chicken dinner party.

Where Gregory's from, fried chicken speaks of traditions and rituals. But fried chicken is not just a dish for special events. Fried chicken *makes* a special event— that's the point. It's humble and egalitarian: everyone is equal when you're eating with your fingers. No pomp and circumstance here. And definitely no tablecloths. This is a party for all your favorite people, the ones with whom there is no need for pretense. Invite them over, make them a drink, and tell them to get involved.

When I was a kid, I used to do a lot of cross-country running. I was never particularly great at it, mind you, and the leaders were usually so far in front I would have to rely on the brightly colored flags tied around the trees to tell me which way to go.

I reckon following recipes without pictures is like cross-country running without the markers. How do you know what you're heading for? So, because this book is full of recipes designed by a chef, specifically for those of us who are not, we've included plenty of pictures to help you get across the finish line.

Most of the recipes are for a party of six; if you have more friends than we do, just make double.

NAOMI HART

GOLDEN
BROWN
DELICIOUS

THE FRIED CHICKEN BRIBE

When Gregory and I moved from New York to Los Angeles, I had to get an American driver's license. By this time I'd been living in the U.S. for nearly six years, but there had never been cause to have one. Who drives a car in New York?!

Isn't it reassuring when you discover that another country does something as badly as your own? I am pleased to confirm that my experience in the American DMV was no less exasperating than what I have endured in Australia. I can guarantee that at both you will come out frustrated, sweaty, and late for whatever activity you have to do next, no matter how much time you allow.

There I stood, waiting in line for half the morning while looking longingly at my coffee that had been confiscated, as there were "no hot liquids permitted while standing on line." Firstly, it's not *on* line, it's *in* line. And secondly, why not? Why *can't* I drink my coffee while waiting in your terminally long line for someone to help me? No wonder they need security guards.

Eventually it was my turn.

"Y'all can take yer written test raaght now, or y'all can come back again on yer own taame. I don't care whatcha'll do, which way or the other, but you'll be waitin' on line all over again if you leave. Don't think y'all can skip out on that," said the woman behind the desk.

Unsurprisingly, I opted to take the test immediately, but this meant no chance to prepare—and therefore no clue about any of the questions regarding driving in the snow. I'm Australian. Snow only exists on a couple of mountains, and is usually heavily subsidized by the man-made variety. It is not a common driving hazard. Kangaroos, yes. Snow? No.

Fortunately, I managed to scrape through, but the pain didn't end there: I was now required to take the road test.

While I sat there in the line of cars, contemplating my reverse park on the wrong side of the road from the wrong seat in the car, the lady ahead of me got out of her vehicle and carried a bucket of fried chicken over to an assessor.

I watched as he put his hands up in protestation and shook his head. But the lady persisted, lifting the lid off the container and pushing it up under his nose. He hesitated, then after taking a furtive look around, dug out a drumstick and took a huge bite.

She had chosen well. He did not look like a stranger to fried food.

The two of them stood there, laughing and licking their fingers, and then they sauntered over to her car, climbed in, and drove off.

I sat there dumbstruck. Fried chicken is hard currency, apparently. I had just seen it used as a bribe.

HARTSYARD FRIED CHICKEN

Part of the appeal of fried chicken is the ritual involved in its preparation. If you chat with someone who grew up with fried chicken—generally an American—they typically start their sentences with: "My mom would always…" or "First you've got to…" or "The only way to do it is…"

Frying chicken is steeped in conventions. We worked through them all to develop our own.

HARTSYARD FRIED CHICKEN COMMANDMENTS

[1] The chicken has to be as moist as possible.

[2] The pieces have to be perfectly, equally seasoned, all in a dynamic crust.

[3] The batter has to be just right—it must not be dripping with grease.

It took us no fewer than eleven trials to get it just right. Now we apply these fried chicken commandments to the fifteen chickens we cook most nights during service.

Every day without fail, the process is the same. As is the recipe. As is the method. That's how chefs behave. They're people of systems. Of order. Of discipline and repetition. At least that's how they are at work.

At home, it's a whole different story…

HOW WE DO IT

The Hartsyard fried chicken is three days in the making. You'd be forgiven for not wanting to spend that long preparing fried chicken for your next party—which is why we've included a "Quick-fire" version on page 30. But in case you're curious, the following pages will explain the routine of the Hartsyard "chicken technician."

This is how it happens at the restaurant.

MONDAY
Butcher and brine the chicken.

TUESDAY
First cooking of the bird, in a warm water bath.

WEDNESDAY
Make the marinade and seasoned flour mixes.
Soak the chicken in the marinade, then coat it in the flour. Repeat this process.
Soak the chicken one more time and store it wet, ready for tonight and tomorrow night's service.

THURSDAY
See Monday.

FRIDAY
See Tuesday and Wednesday.

SATURDAY
Look at the bookings for tomorrow night and prep accordingly.

SUNDAY
Last night of the week. Hope you've prepped enough to make it through…
Have a cold beer at the bar when the night is done!

MAKING THE BRINE

(2 days prior to eating)

Essentially, brining the chicken introduces salinity to the meat, which increases the ability of the protein to hold moisture, therefore allowing the liquid from the brine to be soaked up. This trapped liquid is what makes the flesh plump and juicy.

But it's not for those of us who do things at the last minute. Brining requires some forethought; you need to do it for at least 6 hours.

---

2 teaspoons black peppercorns
2 teaspoons coriander seeds
1½ tablespoons sea salt
1 tablespoon onion powder
1 tablespoon garlic powder
1 tablespoon smoked paprika
1 tablespoon Old Bay Seasoning
    (see glossary)
2 teaspoons chili flakes
rind of ½ lemon, cut into
    long strips
1 garlic clove, crushed

Heat a 2-quart (70 fl oz/2 liter) stockpot until warm, then dry-roast the peppercorns and coriander seeds until fragrant.

Add 4 cups (32 fl oz/1 liter) water and bring to a simmer. Add the salt and stir until dissolved, then add the remaining ingredients and simmer for 20 minutes.

Remove from the stove and pour into a nonreactive container (i.e., plastic or stainless steel, *not* aluminum). Cool to room temperature, then refrigerate. The brine will keep for up to 3 days, but can only be used once.

Makes enough brine for a 3 lb 2 oz (1.4 kg) chicken.

BUTCHERING THE CHICKEN

Initially we found the size of the bird to be an issue, and finally settled on a 3 lb 2 oz (1.4 kg) chicken. The meat-to-bone ratio works, without the bird being too big. Also, three pieces fit perfectly in our fryer basket. We get two servings from each bird—two legs, two thighs, two breasts.

In the South, they often fry the backbone as well, but we decided not to include that. Instead, the carcasses are used to make stock and chicken gravy. Any remaining are given to Naomi's brother to feed to his dog, and Hendra (one of our cooks) uses the chicken wings when it's his turn to cook staff meals.

Rinse the chicken, pat dry, then place on a board, breast side up, with the drumsticks pointing toward you.

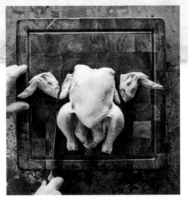

With the legs facing toward you, clip off the wing tips. Reserve these for making stocks or snacks.

Remove each chicken leg quarter through the joint, ensuring the skin covering the breast remains intact.

Turn the bird over and remove the leg quarter, cutting around the socket with a sharp knife to release it.

Now divide each leg quarter into two portions, cutting in between the thigh and the drumstick.

Remove the "crown" (the breast that is still attached to the backbone) by cutting under the breast, down to the wishbone.

For a neater appearance, you can remove the tips of the breast if you wish, and use these in other meals.

Split the two breasts through the breastbone, taking care that both breasts are still on the bone.

There you have it: 3 pounds, 2 ounces of chicken divvied up quite nicely into six lovely portions.

BRINING THE BIRD

Remember, the chicken needs to soak in the brine for at least 6 hours to make it plump and juicy.

Lay all the chicken pieces flat in an appropriately sized nonreactive container.

Pour the cold brine over the chicken pieces, ensuring they are fully submerged.

Cover and refrigerate for a minimum of 6 hours, and a maximum of 12 hours.

FIRST COOKING (1 day prior to eating)

So we've butchered and brined the bird. Now we bundle up the pieces in a vacuum-sealed bag and give it a long, slow soak in a hot water bath. This is the first cooking of the bird.

Remove the chicken pieces from the brine, and leave to drain in a colander. Discard the brine—it will contain bacteria from the raw chicken and should not be used again.

Wash the chicken under cold water and pat dry with a paper towel. Place all the pieces flat (not in a bunch) in a 2-quart (70 fl oz/2 liter) vacuum bag and seal at highest capacity. If using a ziplock bag, remove as much air as possible by sucking the air out through a straw.

Fill a 4-quart (140 fl oz/4 liter) saucepan with 12 cups (105 fl oz/3 liters) of water and heat to a temperature of 147°F (64°C), using a sugar thermometer as a guide. Submerge the chicken pieces in the hot water and cook for 2½ hours.

Remove the bag of cooked chicken and immediately place in iced water until cool. Refrigerate to 40°F (4°C) within 4 hours. If kept sealed in the bag, the chicken can be stored in the fridge for up to 2 days.

MARINATING THE BIRD
(1 day prior to eating)

Buttermilk or no buttermilk in the chicken marinade? Wars have been started over less than this.

The Hartsyard stance is that using buttermilk is the only way to go. The science behind us is that buttermilk contains "aging" enzymes, which break down the chicken proteins and help tenderize the meat.

Traditional buttermilk is the liquid skimmed off the top after butter is churned from cream. The buttermilk we know today is referred to as "cultured" buttermilk, which is actually fermented milk that contains lactic acid. This is why normal milk won't do the trick. Without the lactic acid, you cannot produce the same chemical reaction with your protein, and the chicken will not be tenderized.

Just pretend the chicken is a weary working mother of two. Draw it a deep bath of buttermilk marinade (see below) and leave it to soak for 6–24 hours.

Remove the chicken from its vacuum-sealed bag, then gently wipe it clean of all the cooking liquid and any gelatin with a paper towel.

For the buttermilk marinade, combine 1 cup (8 fl oz/250 ml) Hartsyard Hot Sauce (see page 188) and 1 cup (8 fl oz/250 ml) buttermilk. Pour over the chicken.

Ensuring all the pieces are well coated, cover and refrigerate for at least 6 hours, or up to 24 hours.

A CRUSTY CRUST IS A MUST!

So, the chicken has been brined, vacuum-cooked, marinated, and is deliciously tender. Now it's time to give it a really good crumbing before its final frying.

For a crusty crust, you've got to do the triple flouring process. It's a must. Nonnegotiable.

[1] Soak, coat.

[2] Soak, coat.

[3] Soak, store...then retrieve, coat, fry, eat!

HARTSYARD SEASONED FLOUR MIX

I love Australia, but everything here costs a bucketload. Houses, child care, clothes, Old Bay Seasoning. Back in the U.S., Old Bay Seasoning is $8. Here? $34. THIRTY-FOUR DOLLARS! I refuse to pay $34 for a handful of spices. So we recruited my mom. She's our dealer, our smuggler. A five-foot-nothing, unlikely looking spice trafficker. We've made our own a few times (when she's rudely gone on vacation) and none of the guests seemed to notice, but I reckon the real deal is the best way to go.

Our supply comes every couple of months, often wrapped up in napkins Mom has stitched for the restaurant. She's cunning like that.

2 cups (10½ oz/300 g) self-rising flour
¼ cup (1 oz/30 g) cornstarch
½ cup (3½ oz/100 g) tapioca flour (it is less greasy than wheat flour)
1½ tablespoons sea salt
½ cup (2¼ oz/60 g) onion powder
½ cup (2¼ oz/60 g) garlic powder

½ cup (2¼ oz/60 g) Old Bay Seasoning (see glossary)
2 tablespoons coarsely ground black pepper
1 tablespoon celery salt

Place all the ingredients in a mixing bowl; whisk until thoroughly combined.

TRIPLE FLOURING METHOD

When crumbing the chicken (and unlike how the photos below suggest), it's a good idea to have one wet hand and one dry hand: one hand goes in the marinade, the other hand stays with the flour. And be gentle. Rather than using tongs, which can break through the crust, we suggest using your hands (gloved ones, if you don't know your guests). The third and final flour coating should be done just before the chicken hits the fryer (see next page).

Remove the marinated chicken from the fridge. Place the seasoned flour mix in an appropriately sized container.

Piece by piece, wipe off any excess marinade, retaining the marinade. Dredge the chicken in the flour for its first crumbing.

If the flour bowl is big enough, leave the dredged chicken pieces in the flour; otherwise store them on a plate nearby.

Once all the pieces are coated, return them to the marinade for a second quick soaking, turning to ensure they are well coated in the marinade.

As soon as the chicken has been coated in marinade again, give it a second flouring; this absorbs more moisture and helps create a definite crust.

Coat with marinade a third time. Place on a tray. If frying within 2 hours, leave chicken out of fridge; otherwise chill for up to 12 hours. Give a third flouring immediately prior to frying.

THE GREAT DEEP-FRY DEBATE

Lard versus oil. We know this topic is controversial, but animal lard tastes so good—and for frying chicken, it's the best.

If you don't believe us, and you use oil instead, pick one that's neutral. The last thing you want is your chicken tasting like olives or coconuts. For this reason, most people use some sort of vegetable or seed oil. These also have a high smoke point, which means they can withstand higher cooking temperatures.

But trust us, go for lard. You won't regret it.

NOTE FROM NAOMI: Just in case frying in fat isn't enough for you, if you're frying your chicken in a cast-iron frying pan, Gregory says you might like to consider mounting the lard or oil with 7 tablespoons (3½ oz/100 g) of butter when the chicken is almost done. This introduces a nutty element to the crust and aids in browning.

HARTSYARD DEEP-FRYING CONVENTIONS

- Clean oil is really important for getting the chicken nice and crispy. We use fresh oil every day.

- Your oil temperature needs to be just right. Too cool and your chicken will be greasy and gluggy. Too hot and you'll burn your crust, while the protein stays cold. (Remember, using the Hartsyard method, your chicken will already be cooked.)

- Don't overcrowd your pan or fryer. The oil temperature will drop, the pieces will cook unevenly, and you run the risk of steaming your food rather than frying it.

- Fry the same-sized pieces together. This will help with consistent cooking, as larger pieces require cooler oil to ensure the inside gets properly cooked and heated.

- Don't shake the fryer basket during frying. The crumbs are quite soft, so if you shake the basket (or pan), the crumbs will slide off the chicken.

FRYING YOUR HARTSYARD CHICKEN

We cook our chicken in a deep fryer. If you're using a frying pan instead, go for a deep-sided, cast-iron frying pan, as they're the best for retaining heat. When using a frying pan, be sure to turn the chicken frequently so it cooks and browns evenly.

Before you start, read through the deep-frying conventions on the opposite page.

Bring your chicken pieces to room temperature, and get ready to give them their third and final flour coating by having your bowl of seasoned flour mix at hand.

Next, get your lard or oil sorted. If using a deep fryer, you'll need to fill it with *at least* 4 inches (10 cm) of lard or oil. If using a deep-sided cast-iron frying pan, fill it with *at least* 2 inches (5 cm) of lard or oil.

Heat the lard or oil to 310°F (155°C), using a sugar thermometer as a guide, or until a cube of bread dropped into the oil turns golden brown in 40–45 seconds.

Working in batches so as not to overcrowd the fryer, toss some of the chicken pieces in their third coating of seasoned flour mix and immediately place into the hot oil. It's important not to overcrowd the oil, or the chicken pieces will cook unevenly.

Cook each batch until golden brown delicious: about 11 minutes in a deep fryer, or 15–20 minutes in a cast-iron frying pan.

Remove the chicken from the oil and drain on a paper towel. Serve and eat!

lard or vegetable oil, for
    deep-frying
Hartsyard seasoned flour mix
    (see page 24)

EQUIPMENT
**deep fryer or deep cast-iron
    frying pan**
sugar thermometer

QUICK-FIRE FRIED CHICKEN

So, you don't have the time or energy to spend three days preparing your fried chicken? What's wrong with you? Just kidding. Here's a quick version of the Hartsyard process. You can't fast-track everything, though. You still need at least 2 hours for brining, and another 2 hours for marinating.

BRINING THE BIRD

2 tablespoons granulated sea salt
3 lb 2 oz (1.4 kg) free-range chicken,
  cut into 8 pieces

In a 2-quart (70 fl oz/2 liter) stockpot, bring 4 cups (32 fl oz/1 liter) of water to a simmer. Add the salt and stir until dissolved. Remove from the heat and pour into a nonreactive container (plastic or stainless steel, *not* aluminum).

Cool to room temperature, then refrigerate until completely cold.

Submerge the chicken pieces in the cold brine. Cover and refrigerate for a minimum of 2 hours, and a maximum of 4 hours.

MARINATING THE BIRD

1 cup (8 fl oz/250 ml) Hartsyard Hot Sauce
  (see page 188)
1 cup (8 fl oz/250 ml) buttermilk

In a large bowl, combine the hot sauce and buttermilk. Remove the chicken from the brine and pat dry thoroughly with a paper towel. Place the chicken in the marinade and toss until thoroughly coated.

Cover and refrigerate for 2 hours.

THE CRUMBING MIX

2 cups (10½ oz/300 g) self-rising flour
3 tablespoons Old Bay Seasoning
  (see glossary)
1 tablespoon cayenne pepper
1 tablespoon coarsely ground black pepper
1 tablespoon sweet paprika
1 tablespoon mustard powder
2 teaspoons dried thyme

Mix all the ingredients in a large bowl until thoroughly combined. Have the mixture at hand when you're ready to fry up the chicken.

FRYING THE CHICKEN

18 oz (500 grams) of lard or beef suet

In a cast-iron frying pan large enough to fit the chicken pieces comfortably, melt the lard over medium–low heat. When the lard starts to shimmer, increase the heat to medium.

Remove the chicken from the marinade, then roll in the breading mix to coat. Place back into the marinade, then the breading mix again, then slowly place the chicken pieces into the lard one at a time—they should start sizzling immediately.

Keeping a close eye on the pan and the browning, keep frying until the skin becomes golden on one side. Turn the chicken over and keep frying until a crust has formed and the color is uniform. The whole frying process should take about 12 minutes.

Drain on a paper towel and serve immediately.

MINT JULEP
THE JACK ROSE
DILL PICKLES
SMOKED CAESAR
PORK BELLY CRACKLING
POPPY'S WHISKEY SOURS
PIMIENTO CHEESE SPREAD
MANHATTANS
BEER & CHEDDAR FONDUE WITH MUSTARD PRETZELS
POTATO BREAD
APEROL SOUR
CRAB LOUIE
THE DUCK'S NUTS
PISCO PUNCH
DEM APPELZ
PICKLED WATERMELON RIND
RHUBARB SOUR
VEGETABLE PICKLES
MEMA'S SUN TEA
SWEET ICED TEA
SHRIMP REMOULADE
PLATTER OF CRISPY SKINS & CRACKERS
PICKLED PEPPERS
CHICKEN JERKY
HARTSYARD SODAS
CREAMING SODA
LEMONADE

DRINKS
& SNACKS

MINT JULEP

The mint julep seems simple enough, but its success really comes down to the temperature of the cocktail. Having crushed ice is crucial. You can make your own easily enough at home using your food processor. If, like us, you don't have one, rest assured that manpower will work just fine. Pop your ice into a plastic bag, cover it with a dish towel and, using a meat mallet or rolling pin, take out your frustrations by smashing the ice to smithereens. [Makes 1]

4 mint sprigs, leaves picked,
    plus an extra sprig to garnish
½ fl oz (15 ml) Simple Syrup
    (see page 88)
lightly crushed ice
2 fl oz (60 ml) bourbon

Muddle the mint and syrup in a julep glass. (If you don't have one, any rocks glass or short water glass will do.)

Half-fill the glass with crushed ice. Add half the bourbon and stir to combine. Top with more ice and add the remaining bourbon. Stir again to combine.

Garnish with a sprig of mint and extra crushed ice.

HARTSYARD TWIST
The Hartsyard garden is home to about a dozen different mint varieties, most of which would work well in this drink. For the perfect midsummer cocktail, head straight for apple mint; chocolate mint would do very nicely for an after-dinner occasion.

THE JACK ROSE

There are many excellent theories about the naming of this drink, but the most likely one is also the most obvious and least creative: it's made with applejack, and is rose in color. [Makes 1]

2 fl oz (60 ml) applejack
    (see glossary)
1 fl oz (30 ml) lime juice
½ fl oz (15 ml) grenadine
ice cubes, to serve
½ lime slice, to garnish

Shake all the ingredients over ice cubes in a cocktail shaker and strain into a chilled cocktail glass. Garnish with half a lime slice.

FRIED CHICKEN & FRIENDS

DILL PICKLES

There is nothing better than snapping into a cucumber transformed by a simple mix of vinegar, salt, and sugar. These are an aggressive pickle—salty, slightly sweet, and super sour, with a beautiful garlicky dill undertone. Perfect with fried food or sliced on sandwiches, but also excellent on their own. [Makes about 4 lb 8 oz/2 kg]

Pour the vinegar and ⅓ cup (3½ fl oz/100 ml) water into a 4-quart (140 fl oz/4 liter) stockpot. Add the sugar, salt, and chili flakes and bring to a boil, then reduce the heat and keep at a simmer.

Meanwhile, lay the cucumbers flat in your clean container. Add the garlic, chilies, and severely bruised dill; set aside.

Put all the seeds and spices in a dry-frying pan. Toast over medium heat for about 3 minutes, or until fragrant. As soon as they start to smoke, add them to the simmering liquid, then immediately pour the mix over the cucumbers. There should be enough liquid to submerge all the cucumbers.

Cover the surface of the liquid with parchment paper or plastic wrap to keep the cucumbers from floating above the liquid. Seal the container, then leave at room temperature for 12 hours or overnight.

Refrigerate for at least a week, then snap and enjoy! The pickles will keep in the fridge indefinitely.

4 cups (32 fl oz/1 liter) white vinegar

1⅓ cups (11 oz/310 g) superfine sugar

⅓ cup (1½ oz/40 g) fine sea salt

1 tablespoon chili flakes

2 lb 4 oz (1 kg) Lebanese (short) cucumbers (approximately 12–14), washed and dried

1 garlic bulb, peeled, cloves crushed

3 long green chilies, split lengthwise with the stem on, unseeded

20 dill sprigs, stalks and leaves well bruised with a rolling pin

1 tablespoon black mustard seeds

¼ cup (1 oz/30 g) yellow mustard seeds

¼ cup (1 oz/30 g) whole black peppercorns

1 tablespoon caraway seeds

1 tablespoon fennel seeds

1 tablespoon coriander seeds

EQUIPMENT

1 airtight container large enough to hold all the cucumbers, thoroughly washed with white vinegar and hot water

SMOKED CAESAR

Of course, some grated fresh horseradish to finish would really give this cocktail some extra zing. [Makes 1]

1½ fl oz (45 ml) vodka

3 fl oz (90 ml) Clamato
(see glossary)

½ fl oz (15 ml) smoked tomato
passata (puréed tomatoes;
see note)

1 teaspoon Worcestershire sauce

2 teaspoons Hartsyard Hot Sauce
(see page 188)

pinch of celery salt

ice cubes

lemon wedge, pickles, and
a salami slice, to garnish

Place the vodka, Clamato, passata, Worcestershire sauce, Hartsyard Hot Sauce, and celery salt in a tall glass. Fill with ice cubes and stir.

Season to taste with sea salt and freshly ground black pepper. Serve garnished with a lemon wedge, pickles, and salami.

SMOKED TOMATO PASSATA

To make smoked tomato passata, we simply smoke our tomatoes (see the Charred Peppers recipe on page 142), then purée them. In a pinch, you could use regular tomato passata and add the tiniest droplet of liquid smoke, which you'll find at specialty food stores. Liquid smoke is highly concentrated, so use it drops at a time.

PORK BELLY CRACKLING

When I was living in Puerto Rico, I'd drive home every day along the old road out of San Juan. Lining its side were couples, young and old, selling chicharrón (pork crackling) out of the backs of their cars. The chicharrón came as one long strip, liberally doused in salt, the skin rock-hard with a little bit of flesh and fat on the other side. They served it in a paper bag with a whole lemon. I'd bite the end off the lemon, spit it out, squeeze on the juices, and eat the chicharrón on my drive home. Tasty little snack. The crackling takes a while to prepare, so have a beverage close by— two or three beers should get you over the line. [Serves 6]

Pour the canola oil into a stockpot, leaving 6 inches (15 cm) between the top of the oil and the top of the pot. Heat to 255°F (125°C).

Slowly add the pork pieces, two or three at a time, until all are submerged. Deep-fry for 20–25 minutes, stirring very slowly every 5 minutes, so the pieces don't stick together. Cook until golden brown and crispy, then remove using tongs or a spatula, and drain on a paper towel.

Increase the oil temperature to 400°F (200°C). Return the pork to the oil and cook for another 5 minutes. At this point, the skin will crackle and puff due to the higher temperature. Drain again on a paper towel.

Serve warm, with the shichimi togarashi and sea salt mixed together as a seasoning, and a small bowl of Hartsyard Hot Sauce. Serving with fresh or grilled lemon or lime wedges will not be frowned upon.

4 quarts (140 fl oz/4 liters) canola oil (this sounds like an obscene amount of oil, but it's totally worth it!)

2 lb 4 oz (1 kg) pork belly, skin on, cut into ¾-inch (2 cm) cubes

1 tablespoon shichimi togarashi (see glossary)

1 tablespoon sea salt

Hartsyard Hot Sauce (page 188), to serve (optional)

fresh or grilled lemon or lime wedges (optional)

EQUIPMENT
sugar thermometer

POPPY'S WHISKEY SOURS

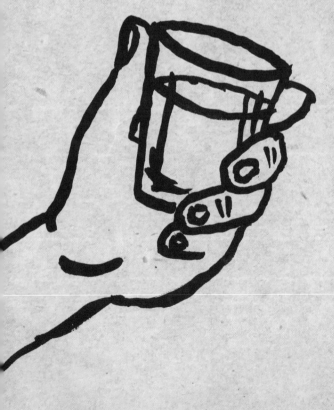
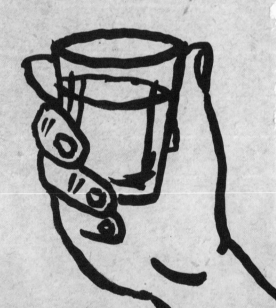

Your first Christmas with your boyfriend's family is an excellent opportunity to make a good impression. You can help with the nieces by reading them bedtime stories. Or you can buy them all tap shoes and cop a round of death stares from their parents as the girls stomp through the wooden-floored house "dancing." You can help your future mother-in-law prepare the potato bake. Or you can get yourself embroiled in a debate about American health insurance with all four of your prospective brothers-in-law.

You can help carry firewood in for the fire. Or you can get absolutely trolleyed on your potential father-in-law's whiskey sours and have to navigate your way to the dining room for Christmas dinner by keeping one hand on the wall at all times.

Before my drinking goggles had blurred my vision, Gregory's parents' house had looked exactly how I'd imagined American houses looked when I'd read *The Baby-Sitters Club* books as a 10-year-old girl—painted brilliant white, with a wraparound veranda, American flag hanging from the porch, a barn out back (white again, with the customary blue trim), a window just perfect for the Christmas tree, smoke billowing from the chimney, and an abandoned bird feeder sitting on the old well, patiently waiting for spring.

I'd happily been inviting myself to different American friends' Christmases for seven years, but this one was different. This one counted. I thought perhaps that I might like to come back to this particular Christmas next year. And every Christmas

after that for as long as I should live. Which makes it even more absurd that I threw caution so far to the wind with my overconsumption of the whiskey sours. Blame it on my nerves. Dinner passed in a blur and we retired to the living room, where Gregory and his four brothers retold tales of their youth while their mother listened in, despair dripping from her ears.

The night finished with me sleeping on the couch in the living room on the ground floor. True, I was likely a little too wobbly to climb the stairs to an actual bedroom, but that wasn't my assigned sleeping space anyway. Gregory and I weren't legally wed at that point, so under his mother's house rules, that meant separate rooms. In fact, it actually meant as far apart as possible without me sleeping in the barn. So Gregory was exiled to the attic, two floors above, and I was given a blanket and assigned the living room couch. No whiskey sour hanky-panky for us.

It should come as no surprise that drinks are really important to Team Llewellyn/Hart, which is why this chapter is positioned where it is, and not buried at the back where you'd usually find it. Who waits until the meal is prepared to have a drink? A huge part of eating food is the convivial surroundings of its preparation. It's why everyone dreams of a kitchen with an island bench and room for at least four stools. Making a cocktail should be the first thing you do.

Just remember who your company is, and drink responsibly.

POPPY'S WHISKEY SOURS

The drink even people who don't like whiskey will love. The frozen ones require minimal effort for maximum effect—mix, pour, and get really, really drunk. Just ask Naomi. For a slightly less dramatic result, use frozen whiskey sour version two. [Makes 1]

BASIC WHISKEY SOUR
1½ fl oz (50 ml) whiskey
    (we prefer a bourbon
    such as Maker's Mark)
1½ fl oz (50 ml) lemon juice
½ fl oz (15 ml) Simple Syrup
    (see page 88)
½ fl oz (15 ml) egg white
1 dash of Angostura bitters
    (see glossary)
ice cubes
1 morello cherry, to garnish
1 lemon slice, to garnish

[MAKES 4]
FROZEN WHISKEY SOUR #1
¾ cup (6 fl oz/185 ml) frozen
    lemonade
¾ cup (6 fl oz/185 ml) frozen
    orange juice
¾ cup (6 fl oz/185 ml) water
¾ cup (6 fl oz/185 ml) whiskey

FROZEN WHISKEY SOUR #2
¾ cup (6 fl oz/185 ml) frozen
    lemonade
⅓ cup (3 fl oz/90 ml) frozen
    orange juice
1 cup (8 fl oz/250 ml) water
½–¾ cup (4–6 fl oz/125–185 ml)
    whiskey

GARNISH
1 maraschino cherry
1 orange slice

To make a basic whiskey sour, put the whiskey, lemon juice, syrup, egg white, and bitters in a cocktail shaker and "dry shake" (see note on page 57) without any ice. Add ice cubes and shake again. Strain into an ice-filled tumbler or rocks glass. Serve garnished with a morello cherry and lemon slice.

To make the frozen whiskey sours, put all the ingredients in a cocktail shaker. Give them a good shake, then pour into any sort of tumbler. Serve garnished with a maraschino cherry and orange slice.

PIMIENTO CHEESE SPREAD

Straight out of the South, straight out of the '70s. This stuff is awesome on Cornbread (see page 151), Waffles (pages 140 and 146), or even just crumbed and fried. It's also perfect in our Crispy Skins and Crackers recipe on pages 79–81, instead of the Vegetable Cream Cheese. [Serves 6]

Process the cheddar cheese in a food processor until finely ground but not pasty. Add the cream cheese and pulse until just combined.

Transfer to a bowl, add the mayonnaise and sour cream, and mix to combine. Add the remaining ingredients and mix again.

The cheese spread will keep in an airtight container in the fridge for up to 1 week.

9 oz (250 g) vintage cheddar cheese

7 oz (200 g) cream cheese, at room temperature

¼ cup (1¾ oz/50 g) mayonnaise

¼ cup (1¾ oz/50 g) sour cream

4 tablespoons pimientos (cherry peppers—found stuffed with cheese in most delis), or Brazilian kiss peppers, hand-chopped

⅓ cup (2½ fl oz/80 ml) Hartsyard Hot Sauce (see page 188)

1 teaspoon coarsely ground black pepper

1 teaspoon salt

1 small dill pickle (see page 37), sliced and chopped

½ garlic clove, shaved using a microplane

1 teaspoon smoked paprika

3 dill sprigs, leaves picked and chopped

MANHATTAN

During the Prohibition era, Canadian whisky was used in this drink. Feel free to use whatever type you prefer. [Makes 1]

1½ fl oz (50 ml) rye whiskey
    or bourbon
⅓ fl oz (10 ml) sweet vermouth
2 dashes of Angostura bitters
    (see glossary)
1 cup ice cubes
maraschino cherry or lemon twist,
    to garnish

Put the whiskey, vermouth, bitters, and ice in a cocktail shaker. Stir, then strain into a chilled cocktail glass.
    Garnish with a maraschino cherry or a lemon twist.

POP-POP'S MANHATTAN MEDICINE

My Pop-Pop was a pretty religious man and never drank during Lent. So come Holy Saturday he'd sit up until midnight, and the second the clock struck, he'd be mixing his "medicine" and toasting the risen Lord. [Makes 1]

3 parts liquor of choice
    (Pop-Pop's was
    Windsor Canadian)
1 part vermouth (Pop-Pop
    used equal parts of sweet
    and dry vermouth)
1 dash of Angostura bitters
    (see glossary)
1 teaspoon maraschino
    cherry juice
1 cup ice cubes
maraschino cherry, to garnish

Put the liquor, vermouth, bitters, cherry juice, and ice in a cocktail shaker. Stir, then strain into a chilled cocktail glass.
    Garnish with a maraschino cherry.

THE HARTSYARD MANHATTAN

On the menu since the day we opened, and unlikely to ever leave, this one combines two of my greatest loves: bacon and Jack. [Makes 1]

For the bacon-washed JD, put the bacon in a nonstick saucepan. Slowly heat the bacon to render the fat. Ideally, you want about 1½ fl oz (50 ml) liquid fat for one 24 fl oz (700 ml) bottle of JD.

Remove 1½ fl oz (50 ml) Jack from the bottle; enjoy it in a Gregory-sized shot! Using a funnel, pour the hot rendered bacon fat into the bottle. Replace the lid and shake. Leave the bottle overnight, or for a minimum of 8 hours.

Place the bottle in the freezer for a while; this makes the fat solidify, making it much easier to remove. Strain the liquid through cheesecloth to remove the bacon fat. Return the Jack to its original bottle, and your bacon-washed JD is now ready to use.

For the candied bacon, preheat your oven to its lowest possible setting—200°F (100°C) or lower. Place your bacon strips on a baking tray and brush with maple syrup. Bake for at least 2 hours, or until the bacon becomes really crispy. Leave to cool and use straight away; alternatively, the candied bacon strips can be frozen in an airtight container for a few days.

To serve, pour a 1½ fl oz (50 ml) shot of the bacon-washed JD into a cocktail shaker. Add the vermouth, all the bitters, the smoked maple syrup, and ice. Stir, then strain into a chilled coupette glass. Garnish with a candied bacon strip.

1½ fl oz (50 ml) bacon-washed Jack Daniel's (see below)
⅓ fl oz (10 ml) sweet vermouth
1 dash of orange bitters
2 dashes of Angostura bitters (see glossary)
1 teaspoon Smoked Maple Syrup (see page 202)
1 cup ice cubes
candied bacon, to garnish (see below)

BACON-WASHED JD (MAKES 24 FL OZ/700 ML)
1 lb 2 oz (500 g) bacon— preferably the fattier cheap pieces, as the aim is to get as much bacon fat in liquid form as possible!
24 fl oz (700 ml) bottle of Jack Daniel's

CANDIED BACON
1 small bacon strip per glass
maple syrup, for brushing

BEER & CHEDDAR FONDUE with MUSTARD PRETZELS

Done badly, pretzels are like chewing on an old boot. Done right, they'll change your snacking world. Here's how you do them right. [Serves 6]

BEER & CHEDDAR FONDUE

2 tablespoons pork fat (see Rendering Fat, page 245)

4 garlic cloves, crushed in their papery skins

2 teaspoons black peppercorns

1⅓ cups (10½ fl oz/300 ml) red or amber ale

7 oz (200 g) cream cheese, at room temperature

7 oz (200 g) cloth-bound cheddar cheese, grated

½ cup (1¾ oz/50 g) Parmigiano Reggiano cheese, grated

2 teaspoons sea salt

1 teaspoon freshly ground black pepper

1 teaspoon chili flakes

pinch of espelette pepper (see glossary)

In a small saucepan, warm the pork fat over low heat. Add the garlic and peppercorns and cook for about 1 minute, until the garlic skins brown lightly and the peppercorns become aromatic. Add the beer, turn off the heat, then let cool to room temperature.

In a mixing bowl, mix the cheeses with a wooden spoon until thoroughly combined. Add the remaining ingredients. Strain the beer mixture into the bowl and mix to combine.

Transfer the mixture to a saucepan. Warm over medium–low heat, stirring constantly until the cheeses have melted and the mixture is smooth; the cheese will be stringy at first, and may separate if the mixture boils. Serve warm, with mustard pretzels (see recipe below).

MUSTARD PRETZELS
(MAKES 12)

1 teaspoon sugar

3 teaspoons dried yeast

4½ tablespoons (2¼ oz/60 g) butter, melted

4½ cups (1 lb 8 oz/675 g) all-purpose flour

3 teaspoons sea salt

2 tablespoons yellow mustard seeds, toasted and crushed

½ cup (3¾ oz/110 g) baking soda

2 egg yolks, whisked

SEED MIX

2 teaspoons poppy seeds

2 teaspoons onion flakes

1 teaspoon garlic granules

1 tablespoon nigella seeds (see glossary)

Combine the sugar, yeast, and 1½ cups (13 fl oz/375 ml) warm water in a mixing bowl. Let stand for 10 minutes, until the mixture starts to bubble and fizz.

Add the butter, flour, salt, and mustard seeds. Using an electric stand mixer fitted with a dough hook, mix until the dough becomes homogeneous, smooth, and elastic; this will take about 6 minutes. Turn the dough out into

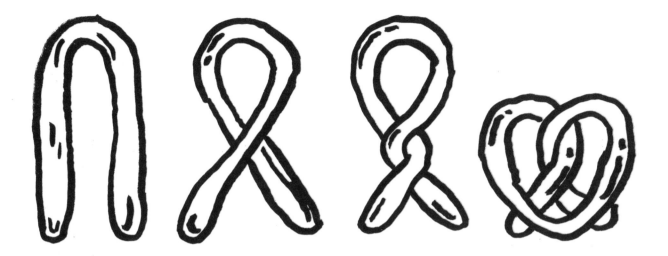

an oiled bowl. Cover with plastic wrap and leave to rest in a warm place for about 1 hour, or until doubled in size.

Meanwhile, preheat the oven to 315°F (160°C). Line a baking tray with parchment paper, and grease with cooking oil spray.

Combine the seed mix ingredients in a small bowl.

In a saucepan, bring 10 cups (87 fl oz/ 2.5 liters) water and the baking soda to a boil.

Divide the dough into 12 equal portions. Roll each piece into a 6-inch (15 cm) length, then shape into a pretzel (see diagram above).

Cook the pretzels individually in the boiling water for 30 seconds each. (The baking soda in the water will gelatinize the flour in the dough; this is why the surface of pretzels and bagels is darker and smoother than other doughs.) Remove from the water and transfer straight to the baking tray.

Brush with the egg yolk and sprinkle with the seed mix. Bake for 15–20 minutes, or until golden and cooked through.

Enjoy warm. The pretzels will keep for a day; just reheat them in a warm oven prior to serving.

POTATO BREAD

Thank you to my grandmother, the original Mema, for this one. She was the best, and so is this bread. [Makes 2 loaves]

3 potatoes, peeled and cut in half

2 eggs, beaten

½ cup (4½ oz/125 g) of your favorite animal fat (see Rendering Fat, pages 244–245)

½ cup (4 oz/115 g) superfine sugar

1 teaspoon sea salt

3 teaspoons dried yeast

5 cups (1 lb 10 oz/750 g) high-gluten flour (often labeled "strong" or "bread" flour)

melted butter, for greasing and brushing

2½ oz (75 g) bag of your favorite salted potato chips, gently crushed by hand

In a saucepan of water, boil the potatoes until tender. Scoop the potatoes from the saucepan, reserving ½ cup (4 fl oz/125 ml) of the cooking liquid.

Push the potatoes through a potato ricer into a bowl. Add the eggs and animal fat. Stir in the sugar, salt, yeast, and reserved potato cooking liquid. Mix in just enough of the flour to make the dough homogeneous, then turn out onto a floured work surface. Knead for 3–4 minutes, or until the dough becomes elastic.

Transfer to an oiled bowl, flip the dough upside down, and cover with a dish towel. Leave in a warm spot for 1–1½ hours, or until the dough has doubled in size.

Remove the dish towel. Punch down the dough. Divide into two equal portions and transfer to two separate greased bread pans, or if you'd like to make individual portions as shown in the photo, divide the dough into twelve 2½ oz (75–80 g) portions and place in small greased bread pans, measuring about 2 x 4 inches (5 x 10 cm). Leave to rise again for about 1 hour.

Meanwhile, preheat the oven to 315°F (160°C).

Brush the top of each loaf with melted butter. Sprinkle with the crushed potato chips. Bake the large loaves for 50 minutes, and the smaller loaves for 25–30 minutes, or until the bread is golden and the chips lightly caramelized.

Turn out the loaves, hot from the oven, onto a wire rack. Allow to cool for 30 minutes before serving.

The potato bread is best enjoyed the same day, but will keep for up to 2 days.

APEROL SOUR

I have issues with runny yolks in my fried eggs, but raw egg whites in this drink don't bother me at all. [Makes 1]

Mix all the orange sherbet ingredients together, adding a little more citric acid if you'd like your sherbet more sour. Lightly moisten the rim of a glass with water, then dip in the sherbet to coat the rim.

Place the Aperol, vermouth, syrup, lemon juice, and egg white in a cocktail shaker and "dry shake" (see below).

Fill the shaker with crushed ice, then give it another vigorous shake. Pour into your sherbet-rimmed glass and serve.

THE "DRY SHAKE"

Always "dry shake" a cocktail that contains egg whites until the egg white is frothy, prior to adding any ice. This extra step ensures the proteins in the egg white have time to get working and create a nice fluffy head on your cocktail.

1½ fl oz (45 ml) Aperol
 (see glossary)
½ fl oz (15 ml) sweet vermouth
1 teaspoon Simple Syrup
 (see page 88)
1½ fl oz (45 ml) lemon juice
½ fl oz (15 ml) egg white
crushed ice

ORANGE SHERBET
1 part citric acid (or more,
 to taste)
2 parts confectioners' sugar
3 parts orange jelly crystals
1 part baking soda

CRAB LOUIE

Everyone thinks you're fancy if you serve crab, but this is such a simple dish to prepare. It's essentially a Cobb salad with crabmeat, and the hardest bit is boiling the eggs. One proviso, though: go fresh and sweet on the crab, and don't be cheap. [Serves 6]

Lay out the crab on a tray, picking out any shells. Add the remaining ingredients except the lettuce and lemon chunks, and mix together until combined.

Cover and chill in the fridge until ready to serve; the salad is best served within a few hours, on a bed of lettuce, with some lemon chunks for squeezing over.

1 lb 2 oz (500 g) jumbo lump crabmeat (see glossary)

½ cup (4½ oz/125 g) mayonnaise (from a jar is fine)

½ cup (4½ oz/125 g) crème fraîche (see glossary) or sour cream

1 teaspoon ground espelette pepper (see glossary)

3 tablespoons thinly sliced chives

2 tablespoons thinly sliced tarragon leaves

4 flat-leaf (Italian) parsley sprigs, leaves picked and thinly sliced

2 tablespoons finely chopped chervil

1 tablespoon Dijon mustard

2 hard-boiled eggs, peeled and grated

juice of ½ lemon

shredded romaine lettuce, to serve

lemon chunks, to serve

THE DUCK'S NUTS

One day I was snacking on peanuts while rendering duck fat to make duck confit when I realized this would be a match made in heaven. Peanuts and duck fat: the duck's nuts! The by-product of rendering fat is crispy duck skin, so we threw that in too...

Don't spend big bucks on buying duck fat; make it yourself and spend the extra money on booze. It really isn't hard, trust me. [Serves 6]

DUCK FAT & CRACKLING
1 lb 2 oz (500 g) duck skin (order this ahead from a good butcher)

Rinse the duck skin thoroughly and pat dry. Place in a stockpot and pour in 5 quarts (175 fl oz/5 liters) of water. Bring to a boil, then cook, uncovered, over medium–high heat for about 30 minutes, until the water has evaporated. The water will break down the skin; the fat will come out of the skin and rise to the surface; the skin will start to brown.

When all the water has evaporated, turn the heat down to medium–low. Using a metal spatula, scrape the skin off the bottom of the pot, as it will want to stick. Continue to render the skin in its own fat until it becomes golden brown delicious; the fat will remain a liquid throughout this process. Remove from the heat.

Remove the skin from the liquid and drain on a paper towel; it will become crispier as it cools.

Leave the duck fat to cool for 15 minutes or so, then strain through a fine mesh strainer to remove any remaining skin.

(If you're not using the duck fat immediately, it will keep in an airtight container in the fridge for up to 1 month. There are lots of uses for duck fat. Spread it on toast, use it for roasting meats and vegetables, frying eggs, in warm vinaigrettes, and of course duck confit.)

Now get ready to serve up the Duck's Nuts!

TO SERVE
1 lb 2 oz (500 g) whole peanuts, in their shells
1 lime, halved
1 tablespoon Togarashi salt (see page 205)

In a large frying pan, heat the duck fat over medium heat for about 8 minutes. Meanwhile, working in batches, fill a ziplock bag with the peanuts in a single layer, then crack the shells with a meat mallet or rolling pin.

Once the duck fat is heated, add the peanuts and fry for about 4–5 minutes, or until aromatic and golden. Peanuts that have fallen out of their shell should be brown.

Using a metal colander (not a plastic one, as it will melt), strain the peanuts over a bowl, reserving the duck fat for further use. (It can be reused twice.)

Put the lime halves in a very hot frying pan or chargrill pan, cut side down. Cook for 30 seconds, or until charred; charring the lime will intensify its flavor.

Season the peanuts with the Togarashi salt. Add the duck crackling and toss together. Serve warm, with the charred lime for squeezing over.

PISCO PUNCH

In his 1889 work *From Sea to Sea*, Rudyard Kipling immortalized Pisco Punch with these words: "compounded of the shavings of cherub's wings, the glory of a tropical dawn, the red clouds of sunset and the fragments of lost epics by dead masters." We couldn't say it any better. [Makes 1]

Brush thin slices of fresh pineapple flesh on both sides with syrup. Spread the slices in a food dehydrator and leave for at least 12 hours to make some dried pineapple wheels for garnishing your drink.

Cut more pineapple into slices about ½ inch (1 cm) thick and remove the skin. Smoke the pineapple on the barbecue in the same manner as the Charred Peppers on page 142; you'll only need one slice per serving, but it's worthwhile to smoke several pieces at once.

Muddle the smoked pineapple in a Boston glass or cocktail shaker. Add the syrup, bitters, pisco, lemon juice, pineapple juice, and some crushed ice.

Shake vigorously, then pour into a chilled, flared cocktail tumbler. Serve garnished with a dried pineapple wheel.

fresh pineapple slices, for garnishing and muddling
½ fl oz (15 ml) Simple Syrup (see page 88), plus extra for brushing
20 drops (1 ml) Tiki bitters (see glossary; measure it out with a dropper)
1½ fl oz (50 ml) pisco (see glossary)
½ fl oz (15 ml) lemon juice
1¼ fl oz (40 ml) pineapple juice
crushed ice

EQUIPMENT
food dehydrator

DEM APPELZ

We had a bit of a cocktail competition a while back at Hartsyard, and this one was the winner. It went straight onto the cocktail list and has been there ever since. All credit to Hartsyard front-of-house manager, Maddison Howes. [Makes 1]

Place the Tuaca, Jack Daniel's, apple juice, lemon juice, and egg white in a cocktail shaker and "dry shake" (see note on page 57).

Fill the shaker with ice cubes, then give it another vigorous shake.

Strain into a coupette glass. Serve garnished with a sprinkling of cinnamon sugar.

1¼ fl oz (40 ml) Tuaca (see glossary)
½ fl oz (20 ml) Jack Daniel's Tennessee Honey
1¼ fl oz (40 ml) cloudy apple juice
½ fl oz (15 ml) lemon juice
½ fl oz (15 ml) egg white
ice cubes
cinnamon sugar, for sprinkling

PICKLED WATERMELON RIND

You won't find this in too many places other than the South. It's the perfect acidic snack to accompany fried foods, particularly chicken. Worth the effort, I promise. [Serves 6]

1 whole small–medium
    watermelon
2 cups (17 fl oz/500 ml) apple
    cider vinegar
½ cup (4 oz/115 g) superfine
    sugar
½ cup (4 fl oz/125 ml) maple syrup
1 tablespoon fine sea salt
1-inch (2.5 cm) knob of fresh
    ginger, unpeeled, sliced
3 basil sprigs
2 teaspoons chili flakes
2 teaspoons black peppercorns
4 star anise
1 tablespoon coriander seeds

EQUIPMENT
1 airtight container large enough
    to hold all the watermelon rind
    strips, thoroughly washed with
    white vinegar and hot water

Wash the watermelon thoroughly, then cut into quarters. Remove the flesh from each portion, leaving no more than ¼ inch (5 mm) of red flesh on the watermelon rind. (Stash the watermelon flesh in the fridge to snack on later.)

Slice each watermelon rind into strips about 3¼–4 inches (8–10 cm) long and ¼–⅜ inch (5–8 mm) wide. Peel each piece, discarding the green skin. Lay the rind strips in an airtight container, then refrigerate.

Pour the vinegar and 1 cup (8 fl oz/250 ml) water into a 4-quart (140 fl oz/4 liter) stockpot. Add the sugar, maple syrup, salt, ginger, basil sprigs, and chili flakes. Bring to a boil, then reduce the heat and keep at a simmer.

In a dry-frying pan, toast the peppercorns, star anise, and coriander seeds over medium heat for about 1½ minutes, or until fragrant. As soon as they start to smoke, add them to the simmering liquid, then remove from the heat. Pour into a container, then cover and refrigerate until cold.

Pour the pickling liquid over the watermelon rind strips; there should be enough liquid to submerge them all. Cover the surface of the liquid with parchment paper or plastic wrap, to keep all the rind strips submerged.

Seal the container and refrigerate immediately (or after you've finished your beer). Leave for at least 24 hours; they are best after 2 weeks. They will keep in the fridge for much longer than you'll be able to resist eating them!

RHUBARB SOUR

When I was a kid, Mom could never add enough sugar to stewed rhubarb to make me want to eat it. As an adult I quite enjoy this tasty, sweet, yet slightly tart beverage. [Makes 1]

1¼ fl oz (40 ml) applejack
    (see glossary)
½ fl oz (20 ml) rye whiskey
1½ fl oz (50 ml) lemon juice
½ fl oz (15 ml) egg white
½ fl oz (15 ml) Simple Syrup
    (see page 88)
1 large tablespoon cooked
    rhubarb (see note)
ice cubes or crushed ice, to serve
confectioners' sugar, for dusting

Add all the ingredients except the ice and confectioners' sugar to a cocktail shaker and "dry shake" (see note on page 57) for 20 seconds.

Add ice to the cocktail shaker and shake vigorously.

Empty the entire contents into a rocks glass and sprinkle with a light dusting of confectioners' sugar.

RHUBARB, RHUBARB, RHUBARB

To cook up some rhubarb, take two healthy-looking rhubarb stalks, trim away all the leaves and any green bits, then cut the stalks into matchstick lengths. Place on a baking tray and sprinkle with ½ cup (4 oz/115 g) superfine sugar and 2 teaspoons pumpkin pie spice. Roast in a preheated 350°F (180°C) oven for 15 minutes, or until soft. Leave to cool, then transfer to an airtight jar. Use any leftover cooked rhubarb as a compote for oatmeal or pancakes.

VEGETABLE PICKLES

These pickles were an accompaniment to our pork terrine, a popular opening-menu item. Eventually I got sick of making the terrine and took it off the menu, but I kept the pickles on as a stand-alone dish, using as much produce from the Hartsyard garden as possible. The vegetables below are just a guide; use whatever ones are available. Tasty additions could include heirloom or breakfast radishes cut into halves or quarters, or sliced into rounds; small cauliflower florets; and turnip, cut into rounds or quarters, depending on size. [Serves 6]

Pour the vinegar into a saucepan. Add the sugar, salt, and 1 cup (8 fl oz/250 ml) of water and bring to a boil. Add half the chili flakes, coriander seeds, and peppercorns. Reduce the heat to a simmer and cook for 5 minutes. Remove from the stove and let cool to room temperature.

Meanwhile, prepare the vegetables, keeping them separate, and place each variety in a sterilized jar or airtight container. Divide the remaining chili flakes, coriander seeds, and peppercorns among them.

Strain the pickling liquid, discarding the solids, and return to a boil. Pour the boiling pickling liquid into each vessel until the vegetables are just covered. Cover with parchment paper or plastic wrap, pushing it down onto the surface of the liquid. Let cool to room temperature.

Remove the parchment paper, cover with a lid, and refrigerate for at least 1 week. The pickles will keep in the fridge indefinitely.

4 cups (32 fl oz/1 liter) white distilled vinegar
1½ cups (10½ oz/300 g) superfine sugar
6½ tablespoons (3½ oz/100 g) sea salt
1 tablespoon chili flakes
2 tablespoons coriander seeds, toasted until fragrant
1 teaspoon black peppercorns, toasted until fragrant

VEGETABLES
1 fennel bulb, topped and tailed, cut in half from top to bottom, then sliced into uniform U-shapes
2 carrots, peeled, then sliced about 1/16 inch (2 mm) thick using a Japanese mandoline
2 celery stalks, sliced into batons

EQUIPMENT
Three 2-cup (17 fl oz/500 ml) jars or airtight containers, thoroughly washed with white vinegar and hot water

MEMA'S SUN TEA

Mom used to make this for us kids all the time in summer. It's the laziest way ever to make tea. We suggest you "put it on" in the morning when you start preparing your fried chicken feast. That way, it will be ready by serving time. Accompany it with strips of lemon rind, slices of fresh lemon, honey, crushed mint leaves, or perhaps a wee shot of gin... [Serves 4]

Place the tea bags (you don't even have to use tea leaves!) in a 1-gallon jug (127 fl oz/3.75 liters). Fill the jug with water, then cover and leave in the sun for several hours until the tea has "brewed."

Fill a glass with ice cubes, cover with sun tea, and sip. That's all you have to do.

4–5 black tea bags
ice cubes, to serve

SWEET ICED TEA

[Serves 4]

Place the baking soda, sugar, and tea bags in a heatproof half-gallon (84 fl oz/2.5 liters) glass pitcher or jug.

Add the boiling water and stir until the sugar has dissolved. Let the tea bags steep in the hot water for 15 minutes.

Remove the tea bags and fill with the cool water. Refrigerate for at least 1 hour, until chilled.

½ teaspoon baking soda
¾ cup (6 oz/170 g) superfine sugar
6 black tea bags
3 cups (25 fl oz/750 ml) boiling water
5 cups (42 fl oz/1.25 liters) cool water

FRUITY TWIST

Add a handful of frozen berries and some big lemon wheels to create a refreshing summery tea. You can also go crazy with fresh herbs like mint, lemon thyme, or lemongrass.

Or go *really* crazy and add vodka!

SHRIMP REMOULADE

Like a shrimp cocktail, except you don't need to bother artfully arranging all the ingredients. It's a plate for lazy dippers. [Serves 6]

16 raw jumbo shrimp, shells and
    heads left on, deveined
grated lemon zest, to garnish

FOR POACHING
½ cup (2¼ oz/60 g) Old Bay
    Seasoning (see glossary)
1 lemon, sliced
2 garlic cloves, crushed
1 bay leaf
2 teaspoons black peppercorns

REMOULADE
1 cup (8 oz/250 g) mayonnaise
8–10 scallions, whites only
    (reserve the green tops for
    another recipe)
2 tablespoons pickled horseradish
    or horseradish sauce
2 teaspoons Old Bay Seasoning
    (see glossary)
1 teaspoon smoked paprika,
    plus extra for sprinkling
2 tablespoons Dijon mustard
2 dashes of Tabasco sauce
½ cup (½ oz/15 g) chopped
    flat-leaf (Italian) parsley
3 tablespoons chopped chives

In a saucepan, bring 8 cups (70 fl oz/2 liters) of water to a boil. Add the poaching ingredients, then reduce the heat and simmer for 10–15 minutes. (The lemon slices will break down and release their flavors.)

Add the shrimp to the broth. Reduce the heat to low and gently poach for 5–6 minutes, or until just cooked. Transfer the shrimp to a tray and refrigerate until cold.

Combine all the remoulade ingredients in a mixing bowl and set aside.

Carefully remove the heads from the chilled shrimp. Peel the shells, leaving the tails intact.

Spoon the remoulade onto the side of a serving plate, then sprinkle with lemon zest and a little extra paprika. Pile the shrimp alongside and serve immediately.

PLATTER of CRISPY SKINS & CRACKERS

Don't be alarmed at how long this recipe looks—much of it is explanation. This amazing snacking platter is worth the work and worth the wait! You'll need to plan ahead, though, as the crispy pig's ears require overnight curing and several hours simmering. The pork and chicken crackers encompass the very best flavors of roast meats, but in crunchy form. If your oven is large enough, you can bake them all at the same time, but the pork skin needs a few hours of simmering first, so make a head start on those. The pickled onions are the perfect accompaniment. It's all about balancing flavors: Yin and yang. Fat and acid. Sweet and sour. Naomi and Gregory. [Serves 6]

CRISPY PIG'S EARS

4 whole pig's ears
1 cup (8 oz/250 g) salt
zest of 2 lemons
4 garlic cloves, crushed
1 tablespoon fennel seeds, toasted
1 tablespoon coriander seeds, toasted
1 tablespoon chili flakes
⅓ cup (2½ oz/75 g) superfine sugar
¼ batch of Hartsyard Seasoned Flour Mix
   (see page 24)
4 cups (2 lb 4 oz/1 kg) lard

STOCK

1 onion, halved
1 carrot, quartered
1 celery stalk, roughly chopped
1 garlic bulb, cut in half horizontally
1 tablespoon fennel seeds
1 tablespoon chili flakes
1 teaspoon black peppercorns

EQUIPMENT

sugar thermometer

Check the pig's ears for any hairs and remove them using a sharp razor. Place the ears in a baking dish. Combine the salt, lemon zest, garlic, spices, and sugar, then pour the mixture over the ears, so they are completely covered. Cover with plastic wrap and cure in the fridge for 24 hours.

Remove the ears from the salt mixture. Rinse under cold running water, pat dry, and place in a stockpot. Add the stock ingredients and 4 quarts (140 fl oz/4 liters) of water. Bring to a boil, then reduce the heat and simmer until the ear cartilage is easily pierced with a knife—usually 2–2½ hours, but no more than 3 hours.

Let the pot cool to room temperature, then refrigerate the ears for 2 hours, or until jellified.

Wipe the ears clean with a paper towel. Slice the ears ¹⁄₁₆ inch (2 mm) thick. Toss the slices in the seasoned flour mix, then leave to sit in a colander for 10–15 minutes.

Meanwhile, heat the lard in a 8–10 quart (280–350 fl oz/8–10 liter) heavy-based stockpot to 350°F (180°C), or until a cube of bread dropped into the oil turns golden brown in 15 seconds.

CONTINUED ON THE NEXT PAGE...

Toss the ear slices a second time in the seasoned flour, shaking off any excess flour. Immediately place into the hot lard, being careful of hot splashes. Cook for 5 minutes, until golden brown delicious, stirring constantly for the first 30 seconds to avoid clumping while frying (clumping = unhappy frying).

Remove with a slotted spoon and drain on a paper towel. The key to success here is to lay the ears out flat while they are cooling.

The crispy ears are great on their own, but even better with the Vegetable Cream Cheese (see opposite page), USA Sauce (page 199), or sprinkled with Dry Ranch Spice (page 204).

PICKLED RED ONIONS

¼ cup (2 oz/55 g) superfine sugar
7 tablespoons (3½ fl oz/100 ml) red wine vinegar
¾ cup (7 fl oz/200 ml) red wine
2 teaspoons fennel seeds
1 teaspoon coriander seeds
1 teaspoon chili flakes
1 teaspoon sea salt
1 teaspoon black peppercorns
4 small pickling onions, sliced into rounds about ¹⁄₁₆ inch (2 mm) thick

Put the sugar and vinegar in a saucepan. Cook over high heat for about 5 minutes, until reduced by half. Add the wine and all the spices, and cook for another 10–15 minutes, or until reduced by half again.

Put the onion in a heatproof bowl and strain the hot pickling liquid over. Quickly cover with parchment paper, pushing it down to retain the heat.

Cool to room temperature, then refrigerate until ready to use. The pickled onions will keep indefinitely in an airtight container.

PORK SKIN CRACKERS

1 cup (8 oz/250 g) salt
1 lb 2 oz (500 g) machine-cut pork skin (order this from your butcher and make sure the fat is scraped off; minimal fat = extra-crispy crackers)

In an 8-quart (280 fl oz/8 liter) stockpot, bring 6 quarts (210 fl oz/6 liters) of water to a boil. Add the salt and pork skin, and reduce the heat to a simmer. Cook, uncovered, for 2–2½ hours, until the skin is translucent and can be easily pierced with forefinger and thumb. Drain in a colander, then immediately plunge into cool water and leave until it is cool enough to handle easily.

Preheat the oven to 315°F (160°C). Grab two baking trays of equal size. Line the first with parchment paper and lay the pork skin out flat on the paper. Cover with another sheet of parchment paper and the other tray. Bake for 1½ hours, checking at 15-minute intervals after the first half hour for even crispness and color.

Transfer the skin to a wire rack and cool to room temperature. Break into crackers when you're ready to serve.

The crackers are best enjoyed fresh, but will keep in an airtight container for up to 3 days.

CHICKEN SKIN CRACKERS

7 tablespoons (3½ oz/100 g) salt
1 lb 2 oz (500 g) chicken skin (ask your butcher for this), scraped of excess fat

In a large saucepan, bring 4 cups (32 fl oz/ 1 liter) of water to a boil. Add the salt and boil until the salt has dissolved. Cool to room temperature, and add another 4 cups (32 fl oz/ 1 liter) of water, then pour into a large bowl.

Discard any visible bloodline from the chicken skin. Rinse under cold running water, then place immediately into the salted water. Cover and refrigerate for no more than 2 hours.

Preheat the oven to 315°F (160°C). Grab two baking trays of equal size. Line the first with parchment paper and lay the chicken skin out flat on the paper. Cover with another sheet of parchment paper and the other tray. Bake for 1½ hours, checking at 15-minute intervals after the first half hour for even crispness and color.

Transfer the skin to a wire rack and cool to room temperature. Break into crackers when you're ready to serve.

The crackers are best enjoyed fresh, but will keep in an airtight container for up to 3 days.

SEEDED MALT BREAD

2 cups (17 fl oz/500 ml) milk
2 tablespoons sea salt
8 tablespoons (4 fl oz/120 ml) extra virgin olive oil
¼ cup (½ oz/14 g) dried yeast
3 teaspoons superfine sugar
4 cups (1 lb 5 oz/600 g) all-purpose flour
¼ cup (1 oz/30 g) malt powder
1 tablespoon nigella seeds (see glossary)
1 tablespoon poppy seeds
1 teaspoon chili flakes

Pour 1 cup (8 fl oz/200 ml) of water into a large bowl. Add the milk, salt, and 7 tablespoons (3½ fl oz/100 ml) of the olive oil. Bring to room temperature, then add the yeast and sugar, but don't overmix. Leave for a few minutes until it starts to bubble and froth.

Add the flour, malt powder, seeds, and chili flakes. Mix to combine, then knead in the bowl for 3–4 minutes. If the dough is slightly sticky, add a little more flour. The dough should be pretty loose and soft, so it will rise properly.

Place the dough on an oiled baking tray, spreading it out evenly. Cover with a dish towel and leave to rest for 30 minutes, or until doubled in size.

Preheat the oven to 345°F (175°C). Bake the dough for 30–35 minutes. Remove from the oven and brush with the remaining olive oil.

This bread is best enjoyed fresh, on the day of baking. Seal up any leftover bread and store in the freezer.

VEGETABLE CREAM CHEESE

2 brown onions
1 large carrot, peeled
1 fennel bulb, trimmed
2 celery stalks, trimmed
¼ cup (2 fl oz/60 ml) extra virgin olive oil
¼ cup (2 fl oz/60 ml) Pernod (see glossary), or other anise-flavored liqueur
4 tablespoons finely chopped dill
4 tablespoons thinly sliced chives
4 tablespoons thinly sliced flat-leaf (Italian) parsley
zest and juice of 3 lemons
1 cup (8 oz/250 g) full-fat cream cheese, at room temperature

Using a sharp knife, dice the onions, carrot, fennel, and celery as finely as possible. (Dicing by hand, rather than using a food processor, helps maintain the "integrity" of the vegetables.)

Heat the olive oil in a saucepan. Sauté the vegetables over medium heat for 8 minutes, or until the onion becomes translucent and the liquid has evaporated. Add the Pernod and cook for another 30 seconds. Remove from the heat, transfer to a bowl, and refrigerate until cold.

Place the herbs, lemon zest, and lemon juice in a large bowl. Add the cream cheese and mix until thoroughly combined. Fold in the chilled sautéed vegetables, and season to taste with salt and freshly ground black pepper.

Any leftovers will last in the fridge for 1 week.

TO ASSEMBLE
Slice and toast the seeded malt bread. Dollop the vegetable cream cheese around a serving plate. Haphazardly add the toasted bread and the pork and chicken skin crackers, then top with the pig's ears and pickled red onions. Garnish with fresh herb sprigs or onion sprouts, or whatever dainty greens you have on hand.

PICKLED PEPPERS

No question as to what type of vinegar to use for these pickled peppers—apple cider vinegar is just right. It's sweet and tart, and tempers the heat of the chili perfectly. You can reserve the liquid the chilies are pickled in and use it as a vinaigrette base, in a brine or marinade, or as a dressing for grilled fish. [Serves 6]

Using kitchen scissors or a sharp paring knife, cut the chilies into ¾-inch (2 cm) lengths, wearing gloves if you're sensitive to chili heat. Discard the stems.

In a saucepan, bring the salt, sugar, and vinegar to a boil. Meanwhile, in a small frying pan, dry-roast the peppercorns and coriander seeds for a few minutes over medium heat until fragrant, then add them to the pickling liquid.

Add the chili flakes and chopped chilies, and reduce the heat to a simmer. Cook for 30 minutes, without allowing the pickling liquid to boil.

Strain the mixture, reserving the pickling liquid. Return the liquid to the saucepan, add the garlic, and simmer for 10–15 minutes, or until the liquid has reduced by half.

Transfer the chilies to a nonreactive container (plastic is fine). Pour in enough pickling liquid to submerge the chilies, then cover them with parchment paper or plastic wrap to keep them submerged.

Refrigerate for 1 week before using; the pickles will keep in the fridge for up to 1 month.

- 1 cup (8 oz/250 g) long red Fresno chilies (see glossary)
- 1 cup (8 oz/250 g) long green chilies
- 10 tablespoons (5½ oz/150 g) salt
- 2½ cups (1 lb 2 oz/500 g) superfine sugar
- 4 cups (32 fl oz/1 liter) apple cider vinegar
- 2 tablespoons black peppercorns
- 2 tablespoons coriander seeds
- 1 tablespoon chili flakes
- 1 garlic bulb, peeled, cloves crushed

CHICKEN JERKY

"This recipe can only be done by people who own a dehydrator," said Naomi. "Who actually owns a dehydrator?" she asked. "Your brother," I replied. Ownership of these devices is not as exclusive as it once was. If you're into camping or like to keep some sneaky snacks in the top drawer of your office desk, this recipe is for you. [Serves 6]

Wrap the chicken breast in plastic wrap, then freeze for 30 minutes or until it's firm to the touch; it's okay if the outside is partially frozen.

Remove the chicken from the plastic. Using your sharpest knife (if you don't have a sharp knife, please buy one for this recipe), cut the chicken lengthwise into slices about ⅛ inch (3 mm) thick. Carefully lay the chicken strips in a single layer in a nonreactive container. Combine the remaining ingredients, pour over the chicken, then marinate in the fridge for 8–12 hours.

Drain off the excess liquid. Transfer the chicken slices to your dehydrator trays, laying them out in single layers. Set the dehydrator to its highest setting, or 150°F (65°C), and leave for at least 12 hours.

Let cool to room temperature, then pack in airtight containers. The jerky will keep for 3–6 months.

9 oz (250 g) boneless, skinless chicken breast, impeccably fresh, trimmed of all fat and sinew
½ cup (4 fl oz/125 ml) white soy sauce (see glossary)
1 teaspoon Meyer lemon juice or yuzu juice (see glossary)
½ teaspoon garlic powder
½ teaspoon onion powder
½ teaspoon espelette pepper (see glossary)
½ teaspoon coarsely ground black pepper

EQUIPMENT
food dehydrator
a really sharp knife

HARTSYARD SODAS

For a homemade Hartsyard soda, pour 1 fl oz (30 ml) of your chosen syrup flavor into a tall glass, add ice cubes, and top with chilled soda water. Syrups are incredibly easy to make. All our syrups start with a simple base of equal parts sugar and water. They will last for months in a sealed container or glass bottle in your fridge.[Makes 4 cups (32 fl oz/1 liter)

SIMPLE SYRUP

2 cups (17 fl oz/500 ml) water
2 cups (1 lb/450 g) superfine sugar

In a saucepan, bring the water and sugar to a boil. Stir until the sugar has dissolved, then remove from the heat. Once cooled, pour into a clean receptacle and refrigerate until required.

VANILLA SYRUP

2 cups (17 fl oz/500 ml) water
2 cups (1 lb/450 g) superfine sugar
1 teaspoon vanilla bean paste

In a saucepan, bring the water and sugar to a boil. Stir until the sugar has dissolved, then remove from the heat.

Once the syrup has cooled to lukewarm, whisk in the vanilla bean paste. Pour into a clean receptacle and refrigerate until required.

GINGER SYRUP

2 cups (17 fl oz/500 ml) water
2 cups (1 lb/450 g) superfine sugar
1¼ cups (250 g/9 oz) fresh ginger, peeled and coarsely grated

In a saucepan, bring the water and sugar to a boil. Stir until the sugar has dissolved. Add a little less than 1 cup (200 g/7 oz) of the ginger and leave to simmer for 45 minutes.

Remove from the heat, then stir in the remaining ginger. Transfer to an airtight container, seal, and leave overnight.

Strain the syrup through a sieve into a clean receptacle. Refrigerate until required.

PINEAPPLE SYRUP

2 cups (17 fl oz/500 ml) water
2 cups (1 lb/450 g) superfine sugar
1 pineapple

Place the water and sugar in a saucepan and stir until the sugar has dissolved.

Cut the thick peel from the pineapple and add all the trimmings to the saucepan. Bring to a simmer and leave for about 1 hour on medium–low heat, keeping it tickin' along.

Strain the pineapple skin syrup, then return the syrup to the pan. Blitz the pineapple flesh in a blender, then strain and add to the pan.

Bring to a boil, then immediately pour into a clean receptacle and refrigerate until required.

CREAMING SODA

We put this soda on the menu to show how a real creaming soda is done. Make an adult version by adding 1 fl oz (30 ml) bourbon (or any spirit of your choosing) when pouring the syrup and cream into the glass. [Serves 1]

Pour the syrup and cream into a glass. Add ice cubes and top with soda water.

Cut a small slit in the cherry and place on the edge of the glass as a garnish.

1 fl oz (30 ml) Vanilla Syrup
   (see opposite page)
½ fl oz (20 ml) whipping cream
   (35% fat)
ice cubes
5 fl oz (150 ml) chilled soda water
1 maraschino cherry, to garnish

LEMONADE

For something different, you can substitute lime, grapefruit, or blood orange juice for the lemon juice. [Serves 1]

Pour the lemon juice and syrup into a tall glass. Top with ice cubes and fill with soda water. Add more lemon juice or syrup according to taste.

1 fl oz (30 ml) lemon juice
½ fl oz (20 ml) Simple Syrup
   (see opposite page)
ice cubes
7 fl oz (200 ml) chilled soda water

OYSTER PO' BOYS
SHRIMP POPCORN WITH SOUR YOGURT DIP
POUTINE
MAC 'N' CHEESE
CRAB CAKES
SMOKED PORK WITH CIDER APPLES
BBQ PIT BEANS
BACKYARD BARBECUED OYSTERS
SMOKED LAMB RIBS

WANTED: PERSONAL KITCHEN EXPEDITER

Every night of the week it hits 5 p.m. and I think, "Dinner. Not you again. Can't you just sod off and come back next week? Do we really have to do this every 24 hours?"

Admittedly, dinner for one adult and two small children is just an exercise in indigestion, but as parenting musts go, cooking dinner seems to be one of them. Which is a shame really, because prior to kids, I spent seven years in the United States eating cereal for dinner and I seem all right.

It's not just because cooking dinner for my children is a fairly thankless task, it's also because I have no clue how to coordinate multiple meal elements to all be ready simultaneously. I am blessed therefore that our eldest considers frozen peas a culinary delight. Yes, as in not defrosted.

The restaurant Gregory and I met at in New York City (he ran the kitchen, I greeted the guests) sat just over 100, but during the season (Thanksgiving through New Year) we did over 500 covers on a Saturday night. Out front in my neck of the woods, it was like trying to politely herd cats. "Your table is ready, sir, right this way. No, ma'am, not you, I'm talking to the gentleman behind you. Yes, the coat check is over there. No, I'm sure your wait won't be too much longer. If you don't mind moving so this guest can get through. You're right, 40 minutes is rather a long time. I am sorry about that."

Out the back, Gregory was expediting into a microphone and holding down the dockets with hockey pucks. ("Expediting" is restaurant-speak for reading the dockets and calling the meals out to the chefs, making sure every table gets what they ordered, how they ordered it, in the order they ordered it in.) Two dockets to every hockey puck. His record was calling seven hockey pucks at once.

In a mix of English and Spanish, his

monologue would go something like this: "Chu Cho! Proximo order. Dame pasta: four pappardelle, two cavatelli, four chittara, five spaghetti, two gnocchi. Orlando [who didn't speak a lick of English]! Dame cuatro bass, cinco salmone, tres pollo. Jimmy! Cuatro fiorentina and cuatro salchicha."

The pasta guys would get the pans ready. Orlando would time the fish with them and the meat was getting cooked and ready to rest. Gregory would try to wait until the docket machine stopped spewing out orders, but if it didn't (as so often happened in the middle of a Saturday night service), he would grab them somewhere in the middle of the stream and start calling. Then he'd keep repeating the orders and watch his team while they cooked, counting the number of fish on the grill, how many pasta pots were going, constantly checking that they weren't missing a dish. Among all that were the two private parties going on upstairs and $2,500 worth of takeout ordered by the neighboring law firm. It's no wonder really, that at the end of service, Gregory used to walk out of those kitchen doors and head straight to the bar for Guinness and a shot of Jack. I need both just writing about it.

A couple of years later, halfway around the world in Sydney, and the words from the pass at Hartsyard sound something like this: "Ordering po' boy, octopus, pig tail, chicken, pork and lamb ribs. Henji! Po' boy in the window at 55, octopus in the window at 10 past. Philly! Fire pig tails at 10, drop the chicken at 20. Stu! Pork and lamb at 30."

Here, since the whole menu is designed to share, the open window into the dining room is crucial. The expediter needs their eyes on the diners at all times. They spy a table of two women and know they'll eat way more slowly than two men. Nondrinkers? Faster again. The expediter knows how long it takes for every single dish on the menu to cook and calls them appropriately. Meanwhile, the station chefs must have a running stopwatch in their heads reminding them what dishes for what order are needed on the pass at what time.

Telling the crew the times Gregory wants the food in the window (other chefs often use the words "pick up") requires them to subtract the cooking time from the end time required and start cooking based on that. "Fire" (or "drop") is unsurprisingly easier, as they don't have to think as much, they just cook. When they're going down (or "in the shit" as they usually say), it is much easier for them to just be told, "Go!"

I am frequently "in the shit" while I cook dinner for our girls and me every night Gregory is at the restaurant. This is usually because on any given evening, I may be dealing with a meltdown from Quinn the toddler, running the bath, bringing in the washing, answering a call from Gregory, chasing the garbage truck down the street because we forgot to put the bins out, yelling as I pass the kids selling chocolates for charity that I really cannot afford to buy any more this week, all while holding Edie the separation-anxiety baby, which means dinner can only involve ingredients I can manipulate with one arm—mushrooms, yes, carrots, definitely no.

What I need is my own personal expediter. Someone to coach me through when to turn the steak, chop the salad, mix the sauce, boil the water. One-armed quiche and tuna surprise could return to the dark holes they belong to. Then the possibilities would be endless…

OYSTER PO' BOYS

The po' boys we serve in the restaurant are a variation on the Louisiana staple, the name being a contraction of its original name, "poor boy." In that neck of the woods, you might also find them filled with roast beef, and typically they're served on a baguette—a French influence from New Orleans. We serve ours on house-made English muffins, with coleslaw. Make a start on this recipe the day before serving, as the oysters need a good long buttermilk soaking. [Makes 4]

Place the oysters in a bowl. Add the buttermilk and hot sauce, and stir to combine. Cover and leave to marinate in the fridge for 24 hours.

Remove the oysters from the buttermilk and drain on a paper towel. Heat the vegetable oil in a large frying pan over medium heat.

Coat the oysters with the seasoned flour mix, then fry in the hot oil until golden brown and crisp on the outside, but still soft and creamy inside—about 45–60 seconds on the first side, and another 30 seconds on the second side. Remove and drain on a paper towel.

To serve, place a hot oyster on a muffin base, add a spoonful or two of coleslaw, and top with the muffin lid. Serve with some more hot sauce.

4 large Pacific oysters, shucked
½ cup (3½ fl oz/100 ml) buttermilk
1 tablespoon Hartsyard Hot Sauce (see page 188), plus extra to serve
approximately 4 cups (32 fl oz/ 1 liter) vegetable oil, for deep-frying
¼ batch of Hartsyard Seasoned Flour Mix (see page 24)
4 English Muffins (see page 147), halved, lightly toasted and buttered
¼ batch of Coleslaw (see page 168)

SHRIMP POPCORN with SOUR YOGURT DIP

Almost every takeout joint has popcorn chicken or shrimp on the menu. This is my literal take on it, served as a snack at the restaurant. Sweet, spicy, and fried, when seasoned perfectly it's something you just can't stop eating, especially when served with a creamy, tangy dip. To me, these flavors together are like eating your first Dorito corn chip. Bliss. The dip also goes well with raw vegetables: something Naomi would do. [Serves 6]

lard or vegetable oil, for pan-frying
7 oz (200 g) popping corn
4 cups (32 fl oz/1 liter) vegetable oil, for deep-frying (my preference is actually lard!)
2 cups (9 oz/250 g) cornstarch
4 tablespoons smoked paprika
2 tablespoons Old Bay Seasoning (see glossary)
1 teaspoon freshly ground black pepper
10½ oz (300 g) raw small shrimp, rinsed and patted dry
zest and juice of 1 lemon
½ cup (4 fl oz/125 ml) melted butter
1 tablespoon Togarashi Salt (see page 205)

SOUR YOGURT DIP
1 gelatin sheet, or 1.4 g powdered gelatin
7 oz (200 g) plain yogurt
zest and juice of 2 limes
1 teaspoon sea salt

EQUIPMENT
sugar thermometer

Start by making the dip. If using a gelatin sheet, soak it in cold water until soft and pliable, then squeeze dry and place in a small saucepan. Add about one-quarter of the yogurt (and the powdered gelatin, if using) and heat gently over low heat until the gelatin has melted and the yogurt is warmed; do not allow to boil. Immediately pull off the heat and transfer to a small bowl.

Add the remaining yogurt, lime zest, lime juice, and salt; combine thoroughly, then cover and refrigerate for at least 1 hour. The dip will keep in the fridge for up to 1 week.

Just before you're ready to serve, add enough fat to a large stockpot to just cover the bottom. Heat until just before smoking point. Add the popcorn and cover the pot. Once the corn starts to pop, turn the heat to low and cook until the popping stops, shaking the pot every 30 seconds or so. Transfer the popcorn to a large mixing bowl and cover with a dish towel to keep warm.

Heat the vegetable oil in a deep fryer or heavy-based saucepan to 330°F (165°C), or until a cube of bread dropped into the oil turns golden brown in 25 seconds.

In a mixing bowl, combine the dry ingredients, then gently mix in the shrimp (ensure the shrimp are dry, as cornstarch doesn't like water). Immediately fry in the hot oil for 4–5 minutes, or until crisp. Drain on a paper towel.

In a serving bowl, mix the lemon zest through the melted butter. Add the shrimp, warm popcorn, and Togarashi Salt. Toss thoroughly to evenly disperse the butter throughout. Drizzle with the lemon juice and serve with the dip.

POUTINE

I like hot french fries. I like celery salt. I like beer. I like beef. This is really my perfect dish... When we first opened, we received a couple angry emails from Canadians living in Australia who were a bit upset that we don't make our cheese curds like the original version dictates—but when has melted cheese ever not been a good option? [Serves 6]

2 lb 4 oz (1 kg) beef shin meat (a whole piece is best, rather than in pieces; on or off the bone is fine)

2 tablespoons sea salt

2 onions, halved

1 garlic bulb, halved

4 celery stalks, halved

2 cups (17 fl oz/500 ml) sherry vinegar

2 cups (17 fl oz/500 ml) red wine

1 quantity Smoked Tomatoes (see page 104)

12 cups (105 fl oz/3 liters) Beef Broth (see page 104)

TO SERVE

2 lb 4 oz (1 kg) ready-to-cook french fries (or buy plain, cooked ones from a restaurant if you're really desperate!)

Celery Salt (see page 104), for seasoning

1 quantity Cheddar Beer Sauce (see page 105)

1 quantity Crispy Spring Onions (see page 105)

fresh celery leaves, to garnish

Place the beef shin meat on a large tray. Sprinkle with the sea salt, cover with plastic wrap, and leave to season in the fridge for at least 6–12 hours.

Preheat the oven to 425°F (220°C). Rinse the seasoned beef under cold running water, pat dry, then place in a roasting pan. Spread the onion, garlic, and celery in a separate roasting pan.

Roast the beef for about 45 minutes, or until it turns a rich, deep brown. About 20–30 minutes before the beef is done, add the vegetables to the oven and roast until golden. You may need to turn the beef and veggies to make sure that all sides are roasted evenly.

Add the roasted onion, garlic, and celery to a 1-quart (140 fl oz/4-liter) saucepan. Pour in the vinegar and wine, and cook over medium–high heat for about 15 minutes, or until the pan is dry and there is no excess liquid left.

Add the smoked tomatoes and cook over medium–low heat for 5 minutes. Stir in the beef broth, then add the roasted beef shin meat. Cover with a lid and cook for 3 hours, or until the beef is very tender and is easily separated with a fork.

Remove the beef from the liquid and place it in a baking dish. Strain the liquid back over the beef, discarding the vegetables. Let cool to room temperature.

Using two forks or your hands, shred the meat, mixing in the gravy until you reach your desired texture. Season to taste with sea salt and freshly ground black pepper. Your shredded beef is now ready for smothering over your fries!

CONTINUED ON THE NEXT PAGE...

BEEF BROTH

2 lb 4 oz (1 kg) beef neck bones
2 garlic bulbs, halved
2 onions, halved
4 celery stalks, halved
2 bay leaves
4 quarts (140 fl oz/4 liters) ready-made beef
    or chicken stock

Preheat the oven to 500°F (250°C). Have a
6-quart (210 fl oz/6-liter) stockpot ready.

Place the bones in a roasting pan and
season with sea salt and freshly ground black
pepper. Roast for about 1 hour, or until the
bones are a rich, dark brown; the fat will
render when they are roasted. During the last
20 minutes of roasting, add the garlic bulbs
and turn the bones so that all sides are evenly
roasted.

About 20 minutes before the bones have
finished roasting, heat a cast-iron frying pan
over high heat for 4–5 minutes. When hot, place
the onion halves in the pan, cut side down, and
char for 4–5 minutes, until blackened. Place in
the stockpot.

Now char the celery in the same pan for
3–4 minutes. (This process of charring the
vegetables will give the broth extra color
and flavor.) Add the celery to the stockpot.

Remove the roasted bones from the oven.
Add the roasted bones and garlic to the
stockpot, along with the bay leaves.

Pour 2 cups (17 fl oz/500 ml) of water into
the roasting pan. Use this water to deglaze or
scrape the browned bits stuck to the pan, then
add the liquid to the stockpot.

Pour in the ready-made stock. Place over
medium heat and bring to a simmer, then leave
to simmer for another 12 hours.

Leave the broth to cool, then strain into
airtight containers. The broth will keep in the
fridge for up to 1 week, or can be frozen for up
to 1 month.

CELERY SALT

1 teaspoon celery seeds
½ cup (¼ oz/10 g) firmly packed dark green
    fresh celery leaves
½ cup (2½ oz/65 g) sea salt

Put the celery seeds in a small, dry frying pan
and briefly toast over medium heat until fragrant.
Tip the seeds into a clean coffee grinder, add
the celery leaves and sea salt, and process
until bright green. The mixture will be aromatic
but moist.

Spread the mixture on a baking tray and
leave out to dry overnight.

Pack the celery salt into an airtight container;
it will keep in the pantry for 2–3 weeks.

SMOKED TOMATOES

14 oz (400 g) can chopped tomatoes

EQUIPMENT
smoking box or hooded barbecue
a handful of your favorite food-grade
    woodchips (never use chunks or pellets)

Set up a smoker or hooded barbecue with your
favorite wood chips. Heat it to 345°F (175°C).

Spread the tomatoes in a wide, shallow
baking dish, so the maximum surface area
will be exposed to the smoke, then hot or cold
smoke them for 1 hour.

The smoked tomatoes will keep in an airtight
container in the fridge for up to 1 week.

CRISPY SCALLIONS
3 large scallions

EQUIPMENT
food dehydrator (optional)
Japanese mandoline

Trim the scallions, removing the green tops and the root ends. Using a mandoline, slice the scallions lengthwise to a ¼ inch (4–5 mm) thickness.

Evenly spread the scallion slices on two dehydrator trays. Dry at 120°F (50°C) for about 12 hours, or until sweet and crispy. (If you don't have a dehydrator, bake them in a convection oven on its lowest setting for 6–8 hours.)

Your crispy scallions will keep in an airtight container in the pantry for a day or two.

CHEDDAR BEER SAUCE
⅓ **cup (2¾ oz/80 g) unsalted butter**
⅓ **cup (1¾ oz/50 g) all-purpose flour**
1 cup (8 fl oz/250 ml) milk
1 cup (8 fl oz/250 ml) heavy whipping cream (38% or more fat)
1 cup (8 oz/250 g) of your favorite cheddar cheese, shredded
1 cup (8 fl oz/250 ml) of your favorite pale ale or IPA
espelette pepper (see glossary), to taste

EQUIPMENT
whipped cream charger (optional)

In a 2-quart (70 fl oz/2-liter) saucepan, melt the butter over low heat. Add the flour and mix thoroughly to combine. Cook for 3–4 minutes without browning. (This mixture is called a *roux,* and is what will thicken our sauce.)

Stir in the milk and cream and cook over medium–low heat for about 5 minutes, or until thickened. Beat out any lumps using a whisk, then add the cheese and stir to combine.

Reduce the heat to low so the mixture doesn't bubble—you're not cooking the cheese, just melting it. This should take about 3–4 minutes.

Using a whisk, add the beer and mix together until thoroughly combined. Remove from the heat. Now taste and season with sea salt and espelette pepper. Is it beery enough? Is it salty enough? Is it peppery enough? These are the questions you should be asking now…

When you're happy with the sauce, pour it into a whipped cream charger and charge with two cream bulbs. (If you don't have one of these gadgets, go and buy one… or you can just use a spoon to ladle it over the beef.)

You will have more than enough sauce for the poutine, but a lot is okay. Any leftovers are great on toast with poached eggs.

TO ASSEMBLE
Gently reheat the shredded beef. Take your french fries and fry 'em or bake 'em. Season the hot fries with celery salt, then divide among two or three bowls.

Top with the shredded beef, cover with the cheddar beer sauce, and scatter with the crispy scallions. Sprinkle with lashings of freshly ground black pepper, garnish with fresh celery leaves, and serve.

MAC 'N' CHEESE

Everyone has their own method for making mac 'n' cheese... and so long as it involves hot cheese, cream, and salt, you'll be just fine. [Serves 6]

Preheat the oven to 325°F (170°C). Grease a 4-quart (20 x 15 cm) casserole or baking dish.

Simmer the cream in a saucepan over medium heat for about 10 minutes, or until reduced by one-third. (A good tip to prevent the cream from overflowing when simmering is to place a metal spoon in the pan during cooking.)

Meanwhile, cook the pasta according to the package instructions until al dente—a little bit toothy, but not chewy.

Strain the pasta, then add to the pan of reduced cream. Cook for another 4–5 minutes, stirring to coat the pasta with the cream. Now add all the cheese and stir to combine. Cook until the cheese has melted and the mixture is thoroughly combined. Stir in the ham, scallion, and chives; the mixture should be creamy, cheesy, steamy. Pour into the prepared baking dish.

To make the topping, warm the duck fat until melted, either in a saucepan or a microwave. Place the remaining topping ingredients in a bowl, pour the melted duck fat over, then gently massage the fat into the ingredients until the texture is coarse, like sand.

Evenly cover the pasta mixture with the topping. Bake for 10–15 minutes, or until the bread crumbs are golden and crunchy.

Sprinkle with extra thyme, then spoon and serve.

4 cups (32 fl oz/1 liter) whipping cream (35% fat)
2½ cups (10½ oz/300 g) elbow-shaped pasta or ditalini
1 cup (3½ oz/100 g) cloth-bound farmhouse cheddar cheese, grated
½ cup (1¾ oz/50 g) smoked Gouda, grated
½ cup (1¾ oz/50 g) Parmigiano Reggiano cheese, grated
1 cup (3½ oz/100 g) smoked leg ham, sliced thickly, then diced to about the same size as the pasta
1 scallion, thinly sliced
⅓ cup (1 oz/25 g) thinly sliced chives

TOPPING
¾ cup (4½ oz/125 g) duck fat (for duck fat, see the Duck's Nuts recipe, page 62; or substitute lard, beef fat, or clarified butter)
1 cup (2¼ oz/60 g) panko bread crumbs
1 garlic clove, grated using a microplane
1 teaspoon coarsely ground black pepper
1 teaspoon sea salt
1 teaspoon smoked paprika
pinch of cayenne pepper
zest of ½ lemon
4 thyme sprigs, leaves picked and coarsely chopped, plus extra to garnish

HOLY SMOKE
A BACKYARD SMOKER!

One night in the very early days of the restaurant, Gregory was smoking broad beans when all of a sudden the grease in the bottom of the machine ignited—and before he could stop it, smoke was billowing out into the dining room, filling everyone's lungs and permeating their hair and clothes.

Frankly, our opening budget was pretty insufficient, so all we could afford at the time was a rickety little homemade smoker that got pounded night after night smoking beans, lamb ribs, pork shoulder, water, sugar, oil, vegetables, seafood, tomatoes, pineapple, syrups… anything, really. Gregory was into smoking in a big way. Now that I think on it, it also coincided with him quitting smoking. Again. Perhaps we can draw a parallel…

That smoker took a real beating, all

day and all night. Last thing before he left, Gregory would put in the pork, then at 6:00 the next morning he'd run downstairs in his boxers to take it out and replace it with something else. The smoker was exhausted, and that particular night it decided to protest, light itself on fire, and cease to function at all.

If we'd had a second to think about it, we would have realized something like that was going to happen with an instrument designed for the occasional home use. Problem was, we didn't have a second. Now we use a proper commercial smoker, and in our first year and a half of business, we went through two of them.

Smoking, despite this story, is not just for the professionals. You, too, can light your kitchen on fire.

No, seriously, my brother built a smoker in our parents' backyard and had much success with his toy, but then he left town again on another of his adrenaline-charged adventures and the smokehouse sat idle in his absence.

Upon his return, he fired it up—and who should come marching out, rather annoyed that her home was gradually filling with billows of sweet smoke, but a very angry, very large funnel-web spider, ready to defend her dwelling with her rather lethal weaponry. Before she leaped at him, my brother caught her in a jar and proceeded to give our then two-year-old (standing barefoot by his side) a lesson in the anatomy of one of the world's most venomous creatures. We found her a home at Taronga Zoo and, as far as we know, she still lives there quite happily, paying her rent with occasional donations of venom.

We were going to show you how to build your own backyard smoker, but then realized our backyard wasn't big enough to do it in, because we rent in Sydney where landlords charge like a wounded bull. There's no room for a smoker because we sacrificed our backyard for a laundry.

A HOMEMADE SMOKER

Long before I met Naomi, I was living in Connecticut and commuting to the city to work. Shifts were long, the train trip made it longer… and yet on my one day off a week, I discovered I was bored. To help kill some time, I decided to smoke a salmon and a chicken and invite a few buddies over for dinner. There was just one thing holding me back—I didn't own a smoker. No matter, I thought, I'll just make my own! And so I did. It was fairly suspect, though, with a high chance of catching fire, so for your own smoking endeavors, I recommend using a Weber grill. The Big Green Egg is also a particularly fine retail alternative, or you could purchase an offset smoker, if you find that you smoke often enough to warrant it.

CRAB CAKES

This dish is an ode to Chesapeake Bay, near where I spent my childhood summers. The crabs there are absolutely incredible—literally covered in a layer of fat. I've never seen crabs like them. Serve these crab cakes right out of the pan, with supermarket white bread (the crappy, not-good-for-you variety) and Vegetable Pickles (see page 71). [Makes 4]

1 lb 2 oz (500 g) jumbo lump
    crabmeat (see glossary)
¾ cup (7 fl oz/200 ml) buttermilk
½ cup (4 fl oz/125 ml) canola oil

CRAB SEASONING
vegetable oil, for pan-frying
1 small red pepper, diced
2 egg yolks, lightly beaten
½ cup (2 oz/55 g) dry
    white bread crumbs
zest and juice of 1 lemon
½ cup (4½ oz/125 g) mayonnaise
1 tablespoon Old Bay Seasoning
    (see glossary)
1½ tablespoons Dijon mustard
1½ tablespoons chopped tarragon
3 tablespoons chopped chives
4 flat-leaf (Italian) parsley sprigs,
    leaves picked and chopped
4–5 dashes of Tabasco or
    Hartsyard Hot Sauce
    (see page 188)

SEASONED FLOUR
½ cup (2½ oz/75 g) all-purpose
    flour
1 tablespoon lemon pepper
    seasoning
1 tablespoon garlic powder
1 tablespoon onion powder
½ teaspoon cayenne pepper
2 teaspoons sea salt

Lay out the crabmeat on a lined baking tray. Working quickly to keep the crabmeat as cold as possible, sift through and pick out any shells. Transfer the crabmeat to a bowl and refrigerate while preparing the crab seasoning.

To prepare the crab seasoning, heat a little vegetable oil in a small frying pan and gently sauté the red pepper for about 5 minutes, or until tender. Tip into a bowl and add the remaining crab seasoning ingredients, mixing well.

Working in additions of 3–4 tablespoons, add the crab seasoning to the crabmeat, *not* the other way around, until all the seasoning is used. The mixture will appear to be moist. Cover and refrigerate for 30 minutes, to let the bread crumbs soak up all the moisture from the crabmeat.

In a bowl, combine the ingredients for the seasoned flour. Pour the buttermilk into another bowl. Work the crab mixture into four balls, packing them lightly. Roll them in the buttermilk just to coat, then dust them with the seasoned flour. Press the balls down, flip them over, then press down again to form patties.

Heat the canola oil in a frying pan over medium–high heat for about 2 minutes. Transfer the crab cakes to the pan; they should start sizzling immediately. Cook for about 4 minutes, or until golden brown underneath. Flip them over and cook for another 4 minutes.

Drain briefly on a paper towel and serve immediately.

SMOKED PORK with CIDER APPLES

You'll need a smoker for this one. The pork is finished with a sprinkling of fennel pollen, which you'll find at specialty food stores. [Serves 6]

To make the sheep's milk cheese, place the yogurt in a piece of cheesecloth or a dish towel, suspend it over a bowl, and let it strain in the fridge for at least 24 hours until thick and scoopable.

The next day, combine the olive oil and fermented chili in a bowl. Season with freshly ground black pepper and mix thoroughly. Reserving the whey (the liquid that has collected in the bottom of the bowl) for pickling the cider apples, use an ice cream scoop to scoop out balls of the strained yogurt, placing them into the oil mixture. Cover and leave to mature and marinate in the fridge for 1 day, or up to 1 week.

Two days before serving, generously season the pork with sea salt, coating all the sides—don't be bashful. We don't measure out the salt, so you don't have to either. Leave the salt on the pork for 12 hours.

The next day, prepare your woodchips and smoker or barbecue to 210°F (100°C), or preheat the oven to the same temperature.

Remove the salt from the pork by washing under cold running water, then pat dry with a dish towel. Smoke the pork for 10–12 hours, or slowly bake in the oven for 6–7 hours, until the meat is easily pulled from near the bone.

Meanwhile, prepare the cider apples. Combine the sugar syrup, cider, and reserved whey in a small bowl. Add the apple wedges, then cover and leave to marinate in the fridge for at least 4–5 hours.

TO SERVE

Pull the pork off the bone, discarding the skin and bones, and arrange on a plate. Dress with the pork fat, smoked maple syrup, and vinegar; the pork shouldn't need any more salt.

Remove the balls of yogurt cheese from the marinade and arrange around the plate. Top with the cider apples, sprinkle with the fennel pollen, and tuck right in.

9 lb (4 kg) pork shoulder, skin on, bone in
lots of sea salt, for sprinkling
½ cup (3½ oz/100 g) pork fat (see Rendering Fat, page 245), melted
generous ⅓ cup (3½ fl oz/100 ml) Smoked Maple Syrup (see page 202)
⅓ cup (2½ fl oz/80 ml) apple cider vinegar
1 teaspoon fennel pollen

SHEEP'S MILK CHEESE

4 cups (2 lb 4 oz/1 kg) sheep's milk yogurt
¾ cup (7 fl oz/200 ml) extra virgin olive oil
3 tablespoons fermented chili paste (from Asian grocery stores)

CIDER APPLES

3½ tablespoons (1¾ fl oz/50 ml) Simple Syrup (see page 88)
generous ⅓ cup (3½ fl oz/100 ml) of alcoholic apple cider
generous ⅓ cup (3½ fl oz/100 ml) whey, reserved from making the cheese (above)
2 apples, peeled and cored, then each cut into eight wedges

EQUIPMENT

oak, birch, and apple food-grade woodchips, or your own favorite combination
smoking box or hooded barbecue

BBQ PIT BEANS

The key to good barbecue pit beans is stuffing as much fat and pork as you possibly can into each dried bean. Check your fridge and throw any leftover barbecued meat into the pot as well, especially the burned ends of brisket, then simmer for a good long time. Regular maple syrup will do just fine here—or you can smoke it, as we do (see page 202). [Serves 6]

The beans will need to soak overnight, and the pork belly needs to cure in a spice mix overnight, so start preparing these the day before.

Put the beans in a container that will hold at least 8 cups (70 fl oz/2 liters). Pour in plenty of lukewarm water, then leave to rehydrate and soften for at least 12 hours.

To prepare the pork belly, first season it liberally with sea salt. Crush the garlic, peppercorns, coriander seeds, bay leaf, and lemon zest together using a mortar and pestle. Rub the spice mix thoroughly into the pork belly; cover and refrigerate overnight.

The next day, preheat the oven to 300°F (150°C). Remove the pork belly from the fridge. Rinse it, then place in a roasting pan with a splash of olive oil and roast for 2 hours. Leave to cool, cut into bite-size chunks, and set aside.

Meanwhile, heat your chosen fat in a large saucepan. Add the bacon and cook over medium heat until slightly brown. Add the garlic and cook until golden, stirring constantly. Once the mixture is golden brown delicious, add the onion and cook for another 5–10 minutes, or until golden brown.

Now stir in all the spices and cook for 2–3 minutes, until fragrant. Stir until all the lumps are dispersed, then add the sugar and stir until dissolved. Add the stock, ketchup, maple syrup, vinegar, and canned tomatoes. Bring to a simmer and season to taste.

Drain the beans and give them a quick rinse. Add them to the sauce mixture with the pork belly. Slowly simmer for at least 2 hours, until the beans are soft; start checking after about 1½ hours.

These beans are fantastic served with Cornbread (see page 151), Smoked Lamb Ribs (page 117), fried chicken, or with toast for breakfast.

1 lb 2 oz (500 g) dried white beans

½ cup (4½ oz/125 g) of your favorite animal fat (see Rendering Fat, pages 244–245)

9 oz (250 g) thick-cut smoked bacon, diced

24 garlic cloves, crushed

2 brown onions, diced

2 tablespoons onion powder

2 tablespoons garlic powder

2 tablespoons smoked paprika

1 tablespoon cracked black pepper

1 tablespoon chili flakes

1 tablespoon ground coriander

1 teaspoon dried chipotle chili

½ teaspoon ground cumin

1¼ cup (9 oz/250 g) dark brown sugar

6 cups (52 fl oz/1.5 liters) pork or chicken stock

2 cups (17 fl oz/500 ml) ketchup

¾ cup (7 fl oz/200 ml) maple syrup

½ cup (4 fl oz/125 ml) apple cider vinegar

14 oz (400 g) can chopped roma tomatoes

PORK BELLY

9 oz (250 g) pork belly

6 garlic cloves, peeled

1 tablespoon black peppercorns

1 tablespoon coriander seeds

1 bay leaf, fresh or dried

zest of 1 lemon

olive or vegetable oil, for drizzling

BACKYARD BARBECUED OYSTERS

Seaweed, burlap sacks, loads of charcoal, a fire pit in the sand on the beach: that's how these guys are traditionally cooked. Here's how to do them on the barbecue and enjoy a beachside pit party in your own backyard. If you're willing to buy a dehydrator, the barbecue sauce chips are a brilliant addition. Drying intensifies their flavor, and the freezing gets the chips crispy, making them easier to crumble. Keep any leftover chips in a ziplock bag in the freezer for next time; they'll keep indefinitely. [Makes 12]

1 dozen of your favorite, most plump, in-season oysters, shucked

BARBECUE SAUCE CHIPS
your favorite barbecue sauce

LEMON CHILI BUTTER
1 cup (8 oz/250 g) butter, softened
2 garlic cloves, finely crushed
1 French shallot, very finely chopped
1 teaspoon chili flakes
1 long red chili, the smallest one you can find, finely diced
1 teaspoon salt
1 teaspoon freshly ground black pepper
2 scallions, thinly sliced
5 flat-leaf (Italian) parsley sprigs, leaves picked and chopped
zest and juice of 2 lemons
pinch of espelette pepper (see glossary)

EQUIPMENT
food dehydrator
hooded barbecue

To prepare the barbecue sauce chips, set a food dehydrator to its highest setting. Line a dehydrator tray with parchment paper, then spread an even layer of barbecue sauce on the paper. Dehydrate for 18 hours, but start checking after 12 hours. The sauce should release itself from the paper; it won't feel wet, but should be tacky.

Freeze the dehydrated barbecue sauce on the parchment paper for about 1 hour.

Now lay another piece of parchment paper on top, then roll a rolling pin over, crushing the dried barbecue sauce into shards. Transfer to a ziplock bag and freeze until required.

When you're set to go, preheat a barbecue to 300°F (150°C). Thoroughly mix together the lemon chili butter ingredients and set aside.

Tear off twelve 12-inch (30-cm) squares of foil and shape each into a rounded doughnutlike ring; the hole in the middle should be smaller than the oysters, so they have a bed to sleep in. Arrange the foil doughnut rings on a baking tray. Take each oyster and loosen the adductor muscle, which attaches the oyster to its shell. Place each oyster, in its shell, on a foil ring, then drizzle the lemon chili butter over each entire oyster.

Using tongs, carefully transfer the foil rings to the barbecue grill. Cook over the flame with the lid closed for 4–5 minutes. (If you don't have a hooded barbecue, you can just stick a large heatproof bowl over them, and cook in batches if need be.) The butter should be melted, the shallot in the lemon chili butter sauce should not be crunchy, and the oysters should be warmed through completely.

Sprinkle the barbecue chips evenly over the oysters. Serve immediately, with cocktail forks.

SMOKED LAMB RIBS

This is one of the first dishes we tested for our opening menu. Initially, all we did was salt the ribs and hot-smoke them with oak and hickory chips, and they were mind-blowing! Since then we've added a mustard-based barbecue sauce glaze, which goes perfectly with the smoked lamb fat. Start these babies at least 8–10 hours before your party, as there are a few stages involved. They're delicious with Cornbread (page 151), Pickled Peppers (page 83), and Vegetable Pickles (page 71). [Serves 6]

Place the lamb ribs in a baking dish or a tray large enough to hold them all.

Sprinkle the salt evenly over all the meat on the ribs. Cover with plastic wrap and refrigerate for at least 12 hours, but no longer than 24 hours. (Leaving the ribs smothered in the salt will season the meat and the fat.)

Rinse the salt off the ribs and pat dry with a cloth or a paper towel.

Preheat your woodchips and smoker or barbecue to 275°F (140°C). Smoke the ribs for at least 8 hours; the fat should be translucent rather than white, and the bones easily removed when testing for readiness.

Remove the ribs from the smoker or barbecue and place on a tray. Allow to cool to room temperature, or cover and refrigerate for up to 2 days, until you're ready to give the ribs their final glazing and roasting.

When you're good to go, fire up the barbecue to 315°F (160°C), or alternatively preheat your oven to 400°F (200°C). Brush the ribs with mustard barbecue sauce, then barbecue or roast for 25–30 minutes, basting with more mustard barbecue sauce every 5–10 minutes, until the fat becomes crispy and the meat is nicely roasted. (If you are reheating the ribs after storing them in the fridge for a day or two, add an extra 10–15 minutes to this final step.)

Serve hot, with your choice of sides.

2 lb 4 oz (1 kg) lamb ribs, in 2 portions
1 cup (8 oz/250 g) salt
approximately 1¼ cups (10½ fl oz/ 300 ml) Mustard Barbecue Sauce (see page 205), for glazing and basting

EQUIPMENT
hickory, oak, or birch food-grade woodchips, or your own favorite combination (never use chunks or pellets)
smoking box or hooded barbecue

SPOON BREAD
PARKER HOUSE ROLLS
HUSH PUPPIES
CREAMED CORN
MASHED POTATOES
DIRTY RICE
CORN FRITTERS
FRANNY'S THANKSGIVING GREEN BEAN CASSEROLE
BUTTERMILK BISCUITS
WAFFLES
CHARRED PEPPERS & CRUMBS
MEMA'S POTATO BAKE WITH CORNFLAKE CRUST
SOURDOUGH WAFFLES
ENGLISH MUFFINS
DIXIE POLENTA
CORNBREAD

SIDES

A lot of the side dishes that appear in this book I recognize as having their roots in the road trip Gregory and I took across America from the West to East Coast before we made the move back to Australia. I bought a huge map of the United States, stuck it to our wall in Santa Monica (where we were living in a tiny beach bungalow after leaving New York City), and we designed our route around the homes of Gregory's chef buddies.

Of course, wanting to show their hospitality during our stay, we were treated to the most incredible meals at the most incredible restaurants, so that by the time we hit Ohio I'm certain duck fat had replaced the blood in my veins.

Parker House rolls (see our recipe on page 125) were the essential accessory to freshly caught lobster off the frosty coast of Maine—beautiful, wild, and the beginning of my obsession with billboards ("Take the US out of my uterUS").

Creamed corn (see page 130) was the tasty little side we had in Lewisburg, Pennsylvania, where I dropped Gregory off at his friend's restaurant and spent the afternoon chasing Mennonites around the countryside.

As we headed south, the weather got warmer and the billboards just kept getting better ("Breast milk is the best milk—eat at Mom's"); mashed potatoes (see page 131) were the perfect accompaniment to the very flat, very manicured, and very religious state of North Carolina. ("Following your friends is easy. Following your heart is brave.")

By the time we got to Florida (alligators, humidity, and lots and lots of retirement villages), Gregory was puffier than a winter ski jacket. His mother took one look at him and put him on the Franny Llewellyn Apple Diet—not widely known or accepted for its nutritional merit, but successful nonetheless. He lost 11 pounds in a week.

Gregory applies a commitment to things unlike anyone I've ever encountered, particularly to food. Forget the tatts and baseball cap; he gives away his profession when he orders every starter on the menu, and most of the sides. I suspect he originated the young folks' acronym FOMO (Fear Of Missing Out). But that's something you don't have to fear, because if you like the sides in this chapter, go right ahead and make them all. Then make sure you invite Gregory to your party; it's the kind of event he'd love.

SPOON BREAD

Say what you mean and mean what you say. My dad taught me that. Spoon bread is bread cooked in a pie pan and served with a spoon. [Serves 6]

6–7 slices day-old/stale bread (preferably a sourdough white bread)

4 cups (32 fl oz/1 liter) whipping cream (35% fat)

2 tablespoons pork fat (see Rendering Fat, page 245)

1⅓ cups (3½ oz/100 g) bacon or cured ham, diced

4 garlic cloves, sliced

2 tablespoons chopped sage

½ rosemary sprig

5 flat-leaf (Italian) parsley sprigs, leaves picked and chopped

1 brown onion, finely diced

generous ¾ cup (7 fl oz/200 ml) milk

½ cup (3¼ oz/95 g) polenta (cornmeal); preferably the real stuff, not the instant variety

6 eggs

2 egg yolks

1¼ cups (5½ oz/150 g) grated fontina cheese

½ cup (1¾ oz/50 g) grated cheddar cheese

4 scallions, thinly sliced

Preheat the oven to 300°F (150°C). Line a nonstick pie pan with parchment paper, then spray the paper with cooking oil.

Lightly toast the bread. When cool, place in a large bowl and break into small pieces. Pour in half the cream to soften the bread.

In a small frying pan with a lid, melt the pork fat over medium heat. Add the bacon and cook until it is slightly browned and the fat has been released. Add the garlic and cook for a few more minutes, until golden brown.

Add the herbs and fry for 1 minute, or until crispy, taking care not to burn them, then add the onion. Cover with the lid and cook over low heat for 5 minutes, or until the onion is translucent.

Pour in the milk and remaining cream, and bring to a simmer. Slowly stream in the polenta, stirring constantly. Cook over medium heat for 5–6 minutes, until thickened. Remove from the heat and leave to cool.

In a separate bowl, whisk the eggs and egg yolks together. Pour the egg mixture over the soaked bread mixture and mix to combine. Add the cheeses and mix again, then add the cooled polenta mixture.

Working with your hands, fold the scallion through; the mixture will look pretty rough, and not quite a dough, but thicker than a batter. Season with sea salt and freshly ground black pepper.

Transfer the mixture to the pie pan. Bake for 40 minutes, or until a skewer comes out clean; start checking at 30 minutes.

Serve hot.

PARKER HOUSE ROLLS

A classic way to break bread. These rolls (pictured next page) are found on most tables in the South, accompanying anything from pork roast to smoked fish to hot, smoky barbecued foods. [Makes 12]

Combine the water, sugar, and yeast in the bowl of an electric stand mixer. Leave for 10 minutes, or until frothy. Add the milk and egg, then the flour, salt, and butter. Beat until smooth and homogeneous.

Spray a metal bowl with cooking oil and turn the dough out into the bowl. Spray the top of the dough with cooking oil, then cover with plastic wrap, pushing it down onto the dough. Place in a warm area in the kitchen and leave to rise until doubled in size—1 to 1½ hours, depending on how warm the space is. (The first proving is the most important, as it establishes how well the dough will rise the second time.)

Spray a high-sided, rectangular baking dish (one at least 1½–2 inches [4–5 cm] deep) with cooking oil. Punch the dough in the bowl to release some of the gas that formed during proving. Turn out onto a floured work surface and cut into 12 rough shapes weighing 2½ oz (75–80 g) each. Without overworking the dough, form the rough shapes into balls, making sure the bottom of the ball is closed up. Place in the prepared baking dish, seam side down.

Spray the rolls with cooking oil. Cover lightly with plastic wrap and leave in a warm spot for another hour, or until doubled in size again until fully proven; the tops should rise just above the dish.

Meanwhile, preheat the oven to 315°F (160°C).

Bake the rolls for 18 to 20 minutes, or until golden. About 4 minutes before the end of baking, brush the rolls with the eggy milk and sprinkle with your choice of seeds, if desired.

Enjoy the rolls warm, fresh from the oven. If you need to reheat them, zap them in a microwave, rather than the oven, to keep them moist.

¼ cup (2 fl oz/60 ml) tepid water
¼ cup (2 oz/55 g) superfine sugar
2 teaspoons dried yeast
1 cup (8 fl oz/250 ml) milk
1 egg
3½ cups (1 lb 2½ oz/525 g) all-purpose flour
2 teaspoons sea salt
scant ¾ cup (5½ oz/160 g) butter, melted

TO FINISH
1 egg, lightly beaten with ¼ cup (2 fl oz/60 ml) milk
sesame, poppy, onion, or nigella seeds (optional)

HUSH PUPPIES

In Australia, Hush Puppies are a brand of sensible shoes. In America, they're a cornmeal fritter, filled with anything from onions to fish to vegetables. The version below is pretty standard, so don't be too scared to improvise. These go tremendously well with Dirty Chicken Gravy (see page 191). [Serves 6]

1 cup (6¾ oz/190 g) polenta (cornmeal); preferably the real stuff, not the instant variety
½ cup (2½ oz/75 g) all-purpose flour
1 teaspoon superfine sugar
3 teaspoons baking powder
½ teaspoon sea salt
1 teaspoon ground espelette pepper (see glossary) or chili powder
¾ cup (6 fl oz/180 ml) milk
1 egg
1 small brown onion, finely diced
8 scallions, thinly sliced, including the green bits
1 small green jalapeño chili, stem removed, then cut in half and very finely chopped
3 tablespoons thinly sliced flat-leaf (Italian) parsley
2 cups (17 fl oz/500 ml) canola oil, for shallow-frying

In a good-sized mixing bowl, combine the polenta, flour, sugar, baking powder, salt, and pepper.

In a separate bowl, whisk together the milk and egg, then add to the dry ingredients, but don't overmix. Add the onion, scallions, chili, and parsley, and stir to combine.

Half-fill a medium-sized, cast-iron frying pan with the oil. Heat over medium heat for 5–8 minutes. Test the heat of the oil by dropping in a teaspoon of batter: it should sizzle when it hits the pan. The oil needs to be hot enough to sizzle the batter, but not so hot that it burns the outside before the inside cooks.

Working in batches, fry up tablespoons of the mixture until golden brown, and then cook just a little bit longer—the hush puppies should be crispy.

Drain on a paper towel, season enthusiastically with sea salt and freshly ground black pepper, and serve.

CREAMED CORN

Growing up, we had "corn Saturdays" where we would pick, shuck, and grate bucketloads of corn from the garden. We'd lay it out all over the driveway and set up stations for each job, then we'd bag it up and freeze it for later. Some of it we ate fresh, and I remember my mom used to always say, "Mmm, mmm, mmm, it's like silk sliding down your throat." [Serves 6]

8 corncobs

7 tablespoons (3½ oz/100 g) butter

⅔ cup (3½ oz/100 g) all-purpose flour

2 cups (17 fl oz/500 ml) milk

2 teaspoons sea salt

½ teaspoon freshly ground black pepper

1 teaspoon ground espelette pepper (see glossary) or chili flakes

½ teaspoon freshly grated nutmeg

¼ cup (2½ oz/65 g) sour cream

1 cup (3½ oz/100 g) grated Monterey Jack or vintage cheddar cheese

Preheat the oven to 315°F (160°C). Grease an 8 x 4 inch (20 x 15 cm) baking dish.

Remove and discard any green outer husks and silky ears from the corncobs. Sit a colander in a bowl large enough to hold it. Using a box grater, grate the corncobs into the colander, grating all the way through to the inner core of the cobs.

Reserve about ½ cup (4 fl oz/125 ml) of the corn milk trapped in the bowl; this is a natural form of cornstarch, which we'll use to thicken the white sauce.

In a saucepan, melt the butter over medium heat, but do not allow it to brown. Add the flour, whisking constantly until combined. Cook for 4–5 minutes; there should be no color.

Add the milk, salt, and spices, and slowly bring to a boil, making sure the mixture doesn't stick to the bottom of the pan. Reduce the heat to low and stir with a wooden spoon until the sauce has thickened—this should take about 10–15 minutes altogether.

Stir in the reserved corn milk and cook for 5 minutes. Add the grated corn and cook until the mixture has warmed through—it should be creamy and homogeneous; don't be alarmed if it's looking dry. Add the sour cream, stir to combine, then immediately turn out into the prepared baking dish. Bake for 30 minutes.

Remove from the oven, sprinkle the cheese on top, then bake for an additional 15 minutes, until the cheese has melted and turned a lovely golden brown.

MASHED POTATOES

I was a lot to handle as a kid, so my Mom used to take the summer holidays as an opportunity to farm me out to different family members, including my Uncle Tom, who lived in the Blue Mountain region of Pennsylvania. He taught me how to fish, mow the grounds of the surrounding cherry farms, and how to make mashed potatoes. The secret is plastic cheese. I know, I know, but forget your purist ideals and use the "plastic" variety. My Uncle Tom knew what he was doing. [Serves 6]

Preheat the oven to 345°F (175°C). Rub the potatoes with the fat, place in a baking dish, and season with sea salt. Bake for about 1 hour, or until a fork can be inserted easily into the flesh. Remove from the oven and leave for about 10 minutes, or until cool enough to handle.

Increase the oven temperature to 400°F (200°C). Cut the potatoes in half lengthwise, then scoop out the flesh, making sure the skins are as thin as possible. Return the skins to the baking dish, laying them cut side up. Bake for an additional 15–20 minutes, checking them after about 10 minutes—they should start to get really crispy.

Meanwhile, put the potato flesh through a ricer, or mash using a potato masher, until the lumps are removed, without making the mash too smooth.

In a large saucepan, heat the milk until almost boiling. Add the potato flesh, stirring over low heat, until the mixture is smooth, homogeneous, and quite thick. In three batches, add the cold butter (chilled butter melts more slowly than softened, so the process will take a bit longer, but the end product is magic). Add the buttermilk, stir, then add the sour cream and cheese. Season with sea salt, being mindful of the salted butter.

Transfer to a serving dish. Crush the potato skins over the top, then garnish with the chives and parsley. Season with coarsely ground black pepper and serve.

1 lb 2 oz (500 g) large waxy potatoes, or other mashing potato, washed and scrubbed

⅓ cup (2¾ oz/80 g) of your favorite animal fat (see Rendering Fat, pages 244–245)

½ cup (3½ fl oz/100 ml) milk

14 tablespoons (7 oz/200 g) salted butter, diced and chilled

½ cup (3½ fl oz/100 ml) buttermilk

2 tablespoons sour cream

4 slices processed cheese

½ cup (1 oz/25 g) thinly sliced chives

6 flat-leaf (Italian) parsley sprigs, leaves picked and chopped

DIRTY RICE

The polite people call this "Southern fried rice." It gets its other name from its "dirty" color, which comes from the ground (minced) chicken livers. This is one of those dishes for which every Southern home has its own version. The one thing that should be standard is that the cooked rice should be at least a day old, so it absorbs more flavors. [Serves 6]

4 fresh chicken livers, trimmed
   of any sinew
2 tablespoons canola oil
5½ oz (150 g) ground pork
1½ cups (12 fl oz/375 ml) chicken
   stock (store-bought is fine)
1 small brown onion, finely diced
2 celery stalks, finely diced
8 garlic cloves, crushed
½ teaspoon ground espelette
   pepper (see glossary) or
   chili powder, plus extra
   to serve (optional)
3½ cups (1 lb 7 oz/650 g) day-old
   cooked medium-grain or
   long-grain white or brown rice
   (*not* freshly cooked)
1 long red fresno chili (see
   glossary), stem removed, then
   thinly sliced, seeds and all
4 scallions, thinly sliced, including
   the green bits

Purée the chicken livers in a small bowl, using a handheld stick blender.

Meanwhile, in a flameproof casserole dish, heat the canola oil over medium heat to just before smoking point (the oil is shimmering, no bubbles = 400°F/200°C).

Add the pork and puréed chicken livers and stir until combined. Continue to cook until the meat begins to brown. Be patient—do not constantly stir, as the more brown the meat is, the more flavorful it will be. Season with salt and freshly ground black pepper, and continue cooking until the mixture is thoroughly browned and granular in texture.

Pour in half the stock, then continue cooking until it has evaporated. Now add the onion, celery, garlic, and espelette pepper, stirring constantly over medium–high heat for about 10 minutes, until the vegetables begin to caramelize.

Add the rice and remaining stock, then cover and simmer for 4–5 minutes, until the liquid has evaporated. Stir the rice, from bottom to top, adding the chili and scallions; these should remain fresh and crunchy.

Season to taste; add extra espelette pepper if desired. Turn out into a bowl and devour.

CORN FRITTERS

Naomi grew up in a small country town, and most of her childhood
involved the Bayliss family, a relationship that's continued into
adulthood—their daughter Amy now works for us at the restaurant, and
is the one responsible for dragging these recipes out of my brain and into
Naomi's computer. To my wife, the Baylisses are like family,
and I'm lucky enough that they've let me in as well.
This dish, made by Amy's mum, Anne, and served at every barbecue
Naomi can ever recall, represents her youth. Without getting too
sentimental, this is why I cook. The nostalgia food builds, the feelings
it inspires, the memories it creates. [Makes 12]

Sift the flour, salt, and pepper into a small bowl. Add the
egg. Using electric beaters, gradually beat in the milk, until
smooth. Add the corn and mix to combine.

Heat about ½ inch (1 cm) of oil in a deep fryer or
heavy-based saucepan over medium heat. Working in
batches, fry tablespoons of the mixture for 2–3 minutes, or
until golden brown underneath. Flip the fritters over and
cook the other side.

Drain well on a paper towel and serve immediately, with
some Pickled Red Onions, a small bowl of USA Sauce, and
a sprinkling of Dry Ranch Spice.

¾ cup (3¾ oz/110 g) self-rising
  flour
pinch of sea salt
pinch of freshly ground black
  pepper
1 egg
⅓ cup (2½ fl oz/80 ml) milk
4 cups (10½ oz/300 g) canned
  corn, drained
vegetable oil or lard, for
  pan-frying
Pickled Red Onions (see page 80),
  to serve
USA Sauce (see page 199), to
  serve
Dry Ranch Spice (see page 204),
  for sprinkling

FRANNY'S THANKSGIVING GREEN BEAN CASSEROLE

If this isn't on your Thanksgiving menu, you aren't American. And yes, it has to be canned soup in this recipe—not enough sodium if you make it yourself. [Serves 6]

2½ cups (20 fl oz/600 ml) buttermilk

1 teaspoon cayenne pepper

2 teaspoons sea salt

2 tablespoons Hartsyard Hot Sauce (see page 188)

2 white onions

canola oil, for shallow-frying

1¾ cups (8 oz/225 g) Hartsyard Seasoned Flour Mix (see page 24)

1½ cans (14 fl oz/400 ml) cream of mushroom soup

¾ cup (6 fl oz/185 ml) milk

4 cups (1 lb 2 oz/500 g) cooked sliced green beans

In a bowl, combine the buttermilk, cayenne pepper, salt, and hot sauce. Peel and thinly slice the onions, keeping the rings intact. Soak the onion slices in the buttermilk mixture for 15 minutes. (The natural enzyme in the buttermilk makes the onion less "aggressive" in flavor, and helps the flour adhere to the onion before frying.)

Meanwhile, preheat the oven to 345°F (175°C).

Heat about 1 inch (2.5 cm) of canola oil in a frying pan over medium–high heat until just shimmering. Drain the buttermilk from the onions. Dredge the onion slices in the seasoned flour mix, then break up into individual rings.

Add the onion rings to the oil, in batches if necessary, and fry for 1–2 minutes, until golden. Drain on a paper towel and season with sea salt.

In a bowl, combine the soup, milk, beans, and half the fried onion rings. Season generously with freshly ground black pepper and mix thoroughly. Transfer to a baking dish and bake for 30 minutes, stirring twice.

Sprinkle the remaining fried onion on top, then bake for an additional 5–7 minutes, or until the onion rings are golden brown. Serve hot.

BUTTERMILK BISCUITS

The biscuits are warm, the honey butter is sweet and salty. These are great for breakfast, but do just as well for a late-night snack with a hot cup of tea. [Makes 6]

Preheat the oven to 350°F (180°C). Spray a baking tray with cooking oil.

In a mixing bowl, combine the flour, salt, baking powder, and baking soda. Rub in the butter with your fingers until pea-sized granules form. Add the buttermilk and mix until just combined; there will be a few floury pockets, but that's okay.

Turn the dough out onto a floured work surface and form into a squarish shape, with a thickness of about 1 inch (2.5 cm). Fold the dough into thirds by turning in the right side, then the left. Pat the dough gently to adhere the layers, but do not compress.

Repeat the folding and patting process until you have nine layers in a square shape.

Cut out six rounds, using a 1½–2 inch (4–5 cm) round cutter. (You may have extra or some offcuts—save these and bake them up too; they're great with butter and jam for breakfast!)

Place the dough rounds on the baking tray and bake for 16–20 minutes, or until golden brown.

Meanwhile, combine the honey butter ingredients.

Serve the biscuits warm, with the honey butter. These biscuits also freeze really well; just reheat them in the toaster oven when you're ready to devour them.

1¼ cups (5½ oz/150 g) all-purpose flour
2 teaspoons sea salt
2 teaspoons baking powder
1 teaspoon baking soda
4 tablespoons (2¼ oz/60 g) cold unsalted butter
1 cup (8 fl oz/250 ml) buttermilk

HONEY BUTTER
7 tablespoons (3½ oz/100 g) unsalted butter, at room temperature
⅓ cup (3½ oz/100 g) honey

BUTTERY BRILLIANCE

For flaky, soft biscuits, use butter. It's the butter that steams during baking and gives such a great result. When butter melts inside a baking biscuit, it produces steam (fat can't evaporate during baking, but water can). The steam reacts with the baking soda and creates a chemical reaction that leavens baked goods.

WAFFLES

Don't let anyone tell you that waffles are just for breakfast. When I was growing up, my favorite meal was when my dad cooked us breakfast for dinner. These waffles are savory, but if you'd like them sweet, just ditch the cayenne and black pepper and add some sugar. [Makes 8, serves 4]

2 cups (10½ oz/300 g) all-purpose flour
2 teaspoons baking powder (to leaven the batter)
1 teaspoon sea salt
1 teaspoon cayenne pepper
1 teaspoon coarsely ground black pepper
2 cups (17 fl oz/500 ml) buttermilk
4 eggs
7 tablespoons (3½ oz/100 g) butter, melted

TO SERVE
crispy fried bacon
Smoked Maple Syrup (see page 202)
sifted confectioners' sugar, for sprinkling

EQUIPMENT
waffle iron

Heat a waffle iron and spray with cooking oil.

Meanwhile, in a mixing bowl, combine the flour and other dry ingredients.

In another bowl, whisk together the buttermilk and eggs, then add to the flour mixture and mix until just combined (don't overmix). Fold the melted butter through until just combined.

Working in batches, pour the batter into the waffle iron and cook until golden, following the manufacturer's instructions.

Serve piping hot with crispy fried bacon, a good drizzle of Smoked Maple Syrup, and a sprinkling of confectioners' sugar.

CHARRED PEPPERS & CRUMBS

This recipe is a bit of a fancy one, as you won't see these peppers at your local supermarket. You should be able to find them at farmers' markets or a specialty food store. They're in season during summer. [Serves 6]

½ cup (3½ oz/100 g) each of Friariello di Napoli peppers, Piment d'Anglet peppers, stavros peppers, shishito peppers, padrón peppers

3½ tablespoons (1½ fl oz/50 ml) sherry vinegar

3½ tablespoons (1½ fl oz/50 ml) olive oil

sea salt, to taste

4½ oz (125 g) of your favorite anchovies (if you can find smoked anchovies, that's even better)

SEASONED CRUMBS
small loaf of sourdough bread

1 cup (9 fl oz/250 ml) extra virgin olive oil

8 garlic cloves, sliced

2 teaspoons chili flakes

1 bay leaf

3 tablespoons oregano leaves

1 cup (¾ oz/20 g) flat-leaf (Italian) parsley leaves

1 cup (1 oz/30 g) basil leaves

zest of 1 lemon

2 teaspoons sea salt

1 teaspoon freshly ground black pepper

EQUIPMENT
barbecue

briquettes or charcoal (optional)

Preheat the oven to 315°F (160°C). To make the seasoned crumbs, slice the bread, place on a large baking tray and toast in the oven for 20–25 minutes, until golden. Cool the bread to room temperature—it should be crusty, and some spots will be dry, but that's okay.

Meanwhile, warm the olive oil and garlic in a small saucepan over medium–high heat for about 5 minutes, until the garlic is golden and crispy, stirring frequently. Add the chili flakes, bay leaf, oregano, parsley, and basil—be careful, as the oil may splatter. Cook for 4–5 minutes, or until the herbs are crisp (not limp). Transfer the mixture to a dish and leave to cool to room temperature.

In a food processor, crumble up the toasted bread. Strain the herb mixture, reserving the oil. Add the strained herb mixture to the food processor and pulse, adding a little reserved oil at a time; keep pulsing until the mixture becomes coarse, granular, and resembles sand. Transfer the mixture to a bowl and add the lemon zest, salt, and pepper. The crumbs will be especially fragrant.

Time to char the peppers. If you have a gas barbecue, preheat it to 400°F (200°C). If you have a charcoal one, light enough briquettes or charcoal to get the barbecue screaming hot.

When the charcoal has burned and is ready (when the charcoal is not black anymore; it is gray or white), spread out an even layer of peppers on the barbecue grill, arranging them by variety, as they will cook differently due to their varying shapes and sizes. Cook the peppers until charred; this should take about 1–2 minutes on each side, depending on how high the grill is elevated above the charcoal. The peppers should be roasted dry—don't put any oil on them.

As the peppers come off the grill, sprinkle them with the sherry vinegar, olive oil, and sea salt to taste. Serve topped with the anchovies and seasoned crumbs.

MEMA'S POTATO BAKE
with CORNFLAKE CRUST

Every year, growing up, we'd have a reunion at the family "bungalow," which was really just a nice name for a massive shed with three tiers of bunks lining the walls, a keg on tap, and an outdoor toilet. Without fail, every year my Mema (grandma) would make this potato bake (pictured on the next page), and I can remember scooping out spoon after spoon of it. It was the only thing I ate. [Serves 6]

Preheat the oven to 300°F (150°C). Spray a 13 x 8½ inch (33 x 22 cm) baking dish with cooking oil and line with parchment paper.

Combine all the ingredients, except the cornflakes, in a large bowl, then season with sea salt and freshly ground black pepper. Pour into the prepared baking dish and sprinkle with the cornflakes.

Bake for 1 hour, or until the cornflakes are crisp and the cheese is gooey and melted. Serve hot.

18 oz (500 g) frozen potato nuggets, thawed
½ cup (1¾ oz/50 g) crispy fried shallots (you can buy these from Asian stores, or fry up your own thinly sliced French or red Asian shallots)
1 cup (8 fl oz/250 ml) cream of chicken soup
1 lb (450 g) sour cream
9 tablespoons (4½ oz/125 g) butter, at room temperature
2½ cups (9 oz/250 g) grated sharp cheddar cheese
3⅓ cups (3½ oz/100 g) cornflakes

SOURDOUGH WAFFLES

Sourdough waffles have a certain tang to them. They can be quite "fruity," depending on how aggressive your fermenting process is.

This recipe does require some prior planning and preparation—the sourdough starter needs to be prepped 4 days in advance, and the waffle batter also needs to sit overnight before using.

It's worth it, though: these waffles are a great accompaniment for fried chicken. Serve with White Sausage Gravy (see page 193) or Smoked Maple Syrup (page 202). [Makes 8, serves 4]

2 cups (10½ oz/300 g) all-purpose flour

¼ cup (2 oz/55 g) sugar

2½ cups (21 fl oz/600 ml) buttermilk

1 cup (2½ oz/65 g) sourdough starter (see below)

2 large eggs, at room temperature

6 tablespoons (2¾ oz/80 g) butter, melted

2 teaspoons baking powder

1 teaspoon sea salt

SOURDOUGH STARTER

1 green apple, peeled, cored, and coarsely chopped; or ½ pear, peeled, cored, and crushed; or ½ cup crushed grapes

2 cups (10½ oz/300 g) all-purpose flour, plus an extra ⅔ cup (3½ oz/100 g)

2 cups (17 fl oz/500 ml) tepid water, plus an extra ⅓ cup (3½ fl oz/100 ml)

EQUIPMENT
waffle iron

Start by preparing the sourdough starter. Put the apple in a bowl, add the 2 cups (10½ oz/300 g) flour and 2 cups (17 fl oz/500 ml) tepid water and mix to combine. Transfer to an airtight, nonreactive container and leave at room temperature for 3 days. The mixture should double in size.

Now you need to introduce "food" to the starter, namely new flour and water. Weigh the starter and discard half. (You can make a fresh starter from the discarded batch by keeping it separate and adding new flour and water to it as well, if you like. It will keep for 2–3 days.)

Add the extra ⅔ cup (3½ oz/100 g) flour and ⅓ cup (3½ fl oz/100 ml) tepid water to the retained starter and mix thoroughly. Leave to mature for another 24 hours—the texture should be almost jellylike and slightly bubbly.

Your sourdough starter culture is now ready to use.

To make the waffles, mix the flour, sugar, buttermilk, and sourdough starter in a bowl until combined. Cover with plastic wrap, pushing it down onto the surface. Leave out on the counter to mature overnight, or for at least 12 hours.

The next day, fold in the remaining ingredients, being careful not to overmix.

Heat a waffle iron and spray with cooking oil. Working in batches, pour the batter into the waffle iron and cook until golden, following the manufacturer's instructions.

Serve piping hot.

ENGLISH MUFFINS

Better than an Englishman's! At Hartsyard, we serve these muffins (pictured on the next page) with our Oyster Po' Boys (see page 97), but they also make an excellent breakfast with jam and butter. [Makes 12]

Preheat the oven to 315°F (160°C).

Combine the milk and butter in a small saucepan. Warm over medium heat until the butter has melted, then pull the pan off the heat and cool the mixture to room temperature.

Pour the mixture into the bowl of an electric stand mixer, then add the yeast and sugar, and mix until dissolved. Leave to rest for 10 minutes to allow the yeast to activate; it should become frothy. Add the egg and flour, then beat until smooth and homogeneous.

Turn the dough out onto a work surface dusted with the polenta. Knead the dough by hand for 2 minutes, dusting with extra polenta if it gets too sticky.

Roll the dough out to a thickness of ¾ inch (2 cm), then cut out 12 rounds, using a 2¼ inch (5.5 cm) round cutter. Place the rounds on a baking tray dusted with polenta.

Heat the canola oil in a cast-iron frying pan over medium–low heat. Working four at a time, pan-fry the dough rounds for about 1½ minutes on each side, or until golden brown delicious on both sides, returning each batch to the baking tray.

When all the rounds have been pan-fried, pop the tray in the oven and bake the muffins for 10–12 minutes, or until they crack slightly around the circumference. (The baking is just to "finish" the muffins, as they have already been cooked during pan-frying.)

The muffins are best enjoyed the same day, but can be doused in butter and toasted in the oven again a couple of days later, if there are any left by then.

1 cup (8 fl oz/250 ml) milk
2½ tablespoons (1¼ oz/35 g) butter, chopped
4 teaspoons dried yeast
2 teaspoons superfine sugar
1 egg
3⅓ cups (1 lb 2 oz/500 g) all-purpose flour
approximately 3 cups (1 lb 2 oz/500 g) polenta (cornmeal), for dusting (preferably the real stuff, not the instant variety)
¼ cup (1½ fl oz/50 ml) canola oil

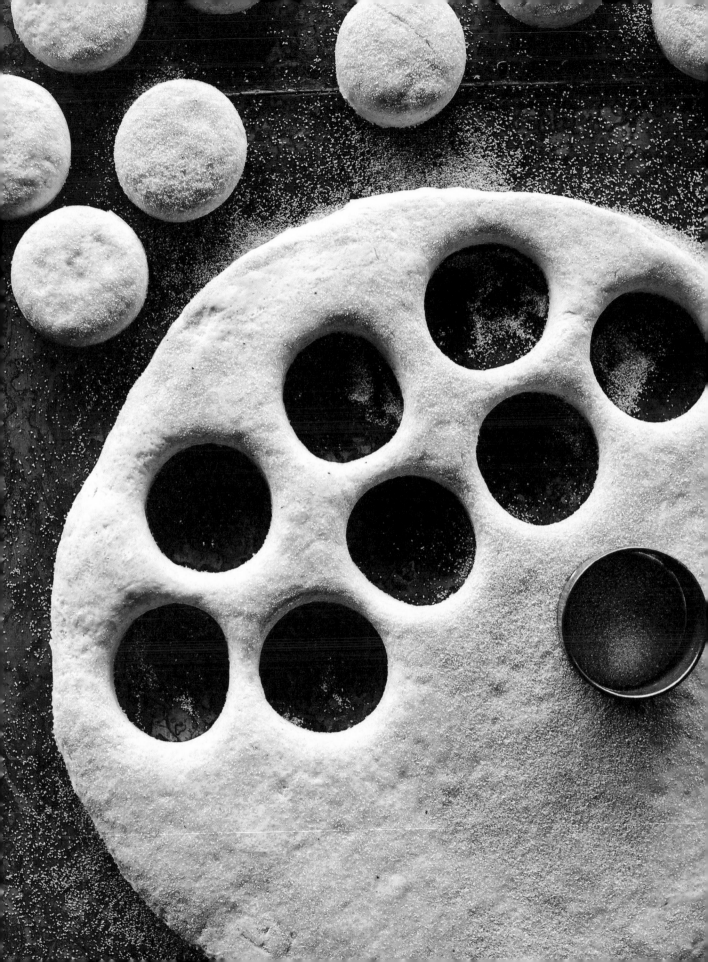

DIXIE POLENTA

This is based on Dixie grits, a staple of the South, which is typically a breakfast dish. This version makes a tasty, cheesy side for a meal at any time of day. [Serves 6]

4 garlic cloves

⅓ cup (2¾ oz/80 g) of your favorite animal fat (see Rendering Fat, pages 244–245)

1 teaspoon chili flakes

5 cups (40 fl oz/1.25 liters) milk

¼ cup (2 fl oz/60 ml) whipping cream (35% fat)

1½ cups (6 oz/175 g) white corn grits (see note)

4 tablespoons (2¼ oz/60 g) butter, softened

1 cup (3½ oz/100 g) grated provolone piccante cheese

½ cup (1¾ oz/50 g) grated cheddar cheese

Peel the garlic and crush the cloves with the back of a knife. Add them to a cold saucepan (a cold pan is best, so the garlic doesn't burn), along with the fat.

Cook over low heat for 3–4 minutes, until the garlic is fragrant and slightly browned. Add the chili flakes, toast for about 1 minute, then pour in the milk and cream.

Increase the heat to medium and bring to a boil, then remove from the heat, and let cool to room temperature. Strain the mixture, discarding the solids, then return the mixture to the same pan over a gentle simmer.

Slowly whisk in the corn grits. Cook slowly over low heat for 30 minutes, stirring often and making sure that the bottom of the pan doesn't scorch.

Whisk in the butter and cheeses until melted and thoroughly combined. Season with sea salt and enjoy!

CORN GRITS

This recipe uses white corn grits—ground white corn, which may be a bit tricky to find in some states. You may be able to buy it online; otherwise, you could buy whole dried white corn kernels and grind them down, or use stone-ground yellow corn instead.

CORNBREAD

Because cornbread doesn't have a lot of flour, it has a tendency to dry out, so serve it hot and fresh, straight from the oven. Slather it in butter and honey, or dip it in meat juices. Sweet or savory, it's a dish that swings both ways. [Makes 12]

Preheat the oven to 345°F (175°C).

Combine the flour, polenta, sugar, baking powder, and salt in a mixing bowl.

In another bowl, whisk together the buttermilk and egg, then add to the polenta mixture, but don't overmix. Stir in the butter; the consistency should resemble a thick batter.

Spoon the batter into a greased 12-cup muffin pan, then bake for 12–15 minutes, or until golden brown. The tops should crack open; you'll know they're done when a skewer inserted in the middle comes out clean. Serve immediately.

1 cup (5½ oz/150 g) all-purpose flour
1 cup (6¾ oz/190 g) polenta (cornmeal); preferably the real stuff, not the instant variety
¼ cup (2 oz/55 g) superfine sugar
1 tablespoon baking powder
2 teaspoons sea salt
⅔ cup (5¼ fl oz/160 ml) buttermilk
1 egg
2 tablespoons (1 oz/30 g) butter, melted

MEMA'S POTATO SALAD
COLLARD GREENS
PICKLED GREEN TOMATOES
FRIED GREEN TOMATOES
BUTTER LETTUCE & DANDELION SALAD
    WITH HOT BACON DRESSING
COLESLAW
CORNCOBS WITH CHARRED CHILI DRESSING
BROAD BEANS ON THE BARBECUE
ROASTED BROCCOLI WITH LEMON JAM,
    WALNUT BUTTER & AGED GOUDA
BRAISED OKRA & TOMATOES
RAW ARTICHOKE & MUSHROOM SALAD
ICEBERG LETTUCE, TOMATO & GRAINS

Gregory calls me a "conversation igniter." He reckons I start people talking and then encourage them to keep going—neighbors, strangers, people you meet in public toilets. That came out wrong. Not people you meet in a clandestine fashion, but the people you encounter because you both get to the hand dryer at the same time. I even manage to talk over the sound of the dryer, which Gregory considers excessive and I consider a testament to the excellent voice training I had while studying musical theater in New York. It makes me perfect for a hostess, as it means my hobby is also my job. I get to chat with every single person who walks in the door, and since I've already bonded with them when they made their reservations, by the time they walk in, we're old friends.

Liking people is an excellent asset when opening a restaurant. As are anonymity and naïveté. I cannot rate those two highly enough. No one knew Gregory. Absolutely no one knew me. Gregory knew nothing about opening restaurants in Sydney. I knew nothing about opening restaurants at all. But he was a chef and I was a hostess, and it seemed like a better option than opening a circus. Although at times I'd argue they're one and the same…

Whenever I try something new, I console myself with the knowledge that I can't possibly be the dumbest person to have ever attempted it. *How hard could this possibly be?* I ask when I'm too far in to quit something and doubt the intelligence of my original decision. It worked for the six years in New York before I met Gregory, when sometimes I would wander about the city poor, lonely, homesick, and once suffering such a serious case of anxiety that I had confused it with long-term food poisoning.

But that was nothing compared with opening Hartsyard, and whenever Gregory floats the idea of a second venue, I flatly tell him that I will consider it when the pain of childbirth actually seems worse than the pain of opening a restaurant.

To be fair, at that point our first daughter, Quinn, was a nonsleeping 16-month-old who had only just stopped using me as a food source, and we lived in a one-bedroom apartment. So, seven weeks into the restaurant opening, we tried to improve the situation by moving out of the one-bedroom apartment into a bigger one directly above the restaurant.

There are no words to adequately express the stupidity of such timing. The movers turned up and kindly pointed out that we hadn't packed a thing. They also noted that we had nothing to pack anything into. Then they took out the recycling.

The single, solitary, positive outcome from that disastrous relocation was the proximity to the coffee machine in the restaurant below, which I visited each morning with my pre-dawn friend. Both of us still in our pajamas, Q would stand at the window and wave at the passing commuters while I brewed a triple-shot latte. Then we'd climb back up the stairs and spend the next hour ringing in the dawn hanging out the restaurant napkins on the washing line we'd jerry-rigged above the kitchen below.

Every day I'd wrangle the mighty Q (park, crafting, singing, swimming—repeat until exhaustion), and if she ever napped, I'd dive for the computer to confirm the night's reservations, answer emails, or pay invoices. When you're overly tired, your brain decides which details are important and which ones aren't. This does not always work in your favor. Being behind in the housework is fine. Incorrectly paying the invoices is not. In my defense, I used to perform for a living. Dancers only have to count to eight.

Each evening my parents would arrive to watch Q, and I would charge down the spiral staircase, leaving them to bathe her in a plastic tub, as the apartment didn't have a bath, and then to sit on the cold, hard floor, as our secondhand couch had been too wide to fit through the narrow doors. Gregory and I were living on warm breakfast cereal and bacon, but we spared my parents that fate and would run up the stairs with a couple of po' boys and sweeten the whole appalling deal with a decent bottle of wine. If they were unavailable, I roped in one of my brothers or a friend—one of them promising only to stop Q lighting herself on fire. In the scheme of things, this seemed like a reasonable objective.

The business of working and mothering is utter bollocks, and I cannot believe women are willing to share tales of their displaced pelvic floor—but nobody tells you that more destructive than any baby exploding through your nether regions is the guilt associated with being a working mum. The distress I felt leaving Q each night (even though all I missed were the notoriously painful events of dinner, bath, and bed) fueled me like nothing else. Gregory had Red Bull. I had mother guilt.

When Gregory and I worked in LA, Gregory had a notice board stuck up in the staff area. It was filled with pictures of the *Los Angeles Times* food critic S. Irene Virbila in all her various disguises. Sydney critics didn't need a disguise with me; I didn't know what they looked like in the first place, and it never occurred to us that they might come in. I vaguely knew the appearance of the big hitters, but newspapers have a budget like the one for opening Hartsyard (vastly inadequate), and their pictures were not up to date.

"Someone who looks like the woman who didn't win *MasterChef* is sitting at the bar with a guy who I'm sure is familiar too," I would say to Gregory, and one of the kitchen guys would Google them and let us know just who we were dealing with.

I got savvy with the bloggers, too. "Can you tell me the temperature Gregory cooks the chicken at, please?" was a request I put to Gregory in our opening week. I could have just told them he would now use the steam that was pouring from his ears.

"Best you email me later," I started saying diplomatically.

Every night people would arrive, certain they had a reservation despite my book saying the opposite. It was several months before I realized we'd been sabotaged by the phone company, who had given us a complimentary voicemail service that we didn't know existed.

Owing to a slow boat from China, we had no chairs for the opening week, aprons were almost out of the budget, and while these days we get compliments for our music (all done by Mark in front of house), back then the playlist consisted of Gregory's angry rock music and love ballads to which I used to teach singing.

In the States, during a run of the musical *Beauty and the Beast*, I was onstage one night listening to the overture when I realized I had completely forgotten to put on my mike. Back to the dressing room I sprinted, ripped off my corset and wig, dragged the mike cord up through my knickers and bra, over my wig cap and into place, hoisted the costume up, sprinted back through the darkened corridors, and skidded into place just as the lights came up for my solo.

Nightly service at a restaurant is really no different. At 5:20 p.m. the bartender can discover the new keg is sour, a waitress gets stuck on a broken-down bus, someone spills the night's supply of hot sauce all over the cool-room floor, and you realize you forgot to wash the napkins. And so, in those frantic ten minutes before you must open the door, the bartender sprints to the store to buy as many six-packs as she can carry, your friend down the street agrees to wait tables in between breastfeeding her newborn, the remaining hot sauce is salvaged and rationed out per table, and you use your daughter's leftover party napkins as serviettes.

Fake it 'til you make it, people.

That, and surround yourself with people you like, who all like what you're doing, and then just go for it.

And several years in now, that's exactly what we're all still doing.

MEMA'S POTATO SALAD

One of my first memories is of my Mema making the dressing for this salad on the crappy old electric stove at our family cabin in the woods. She kept moving the dressing off the stove, and when I asked her why, she explained, "To stop the eggs from scrambling." Everyone needs a potato salad recipe for when they're invited to a picnic, and this one is it. It's by no means fancy, but it's great. Thanks, Mema. [Serves 6]

1 lb 2 oz (500 g) Dutch cream
    or sebago potatoes,
    scrubbed thoroughly
1 bay leaf
3 garlic cloves, crushed
    (fine to leave the skin on)
2 tablespoons sea salt
1 tablespoon black peppercorns
4 thyme sprigs
3 tablespoons chopped chives
4 French shallots, diced
2 tablespoons pickled
    horseradish, or horseradish
    sauce
2 tablespoons Dijon mustard
3 tablespoons Kewpie
    mayonnaise (see glossary)

RED WINE VINEGAR &
    EGG DRESSING
½ cup (4 fl oz/125 ml)
    red wine vinegar
½ cup (3¼ oz/110 g) sugar
2 eggs
2 teaspoons sea salt
1 teaspoon freshly ground
    black pepper

Place the whole potatoes in a stockpot and cover with 12 cups (105 fl oz/3 liters) of water. Add the bay leaf, garlic, salt, peppercorns, and thyme. Bring to a boil, then reduce the heat and simmer for about 30 minutes, or until the potatoes are just cooked—they should be easily pierced with a knife, but not at all mushy, so they will hold their shape in the salad.

Remove the pot from the heat and leave the potatoes in the water for about 10–15 minutes.

Drain and peel the potatoes. Cut each one lengthwise into eight wedges, to give lots of surface area for the dressing to coat. Place in a serving bowl.

Get cracking on the dressing. In a saucepan, bring some water to a simmer. Combine all the dressing ingredients in a heatproof bowl, then place on top of the simmering pan, ensuring that the base of the bowl doesn't touch the water. Cook, stirring frequently, for about 45 seconds, until the eggs have thickened (the yolks will cook).

Immediately pour the dressing over the warm potatoes. Add the chives, shallots, horseradish, mustard, and mayonnaise, then toss together and serve.

COLLARD GREENS

One of my favorite things is the liquid left behind after these babies have been braised. In the South they call it "pot likker." It's garlicky, sulfuric, rich, and sticky. It's good. [Serves 6]

In a medium-sized stockpot, heat the duck fat and bacon over high heat. Cook the bacon for about 5 minutes, until crispy. Add the garlic and chili and cook for 3–5 minutes, until the garlic is golden brown and aromatic. Add the onion and pepper, then cover and cook for 10 minutes, until the onion has caramelized.

Reduce the heat to medium. Add the kale and mustard greens, and stir to combine. Cover the pot and simmer for about 5 minutes, until all the liquid has released from the greens (the greens will discolor). Remove the lid and continue simmering for another 5 minutes, until the greens are wilted and the pan is dry.

Add the vinegar and cook for about 3 minutes, until it has evaporated. Pour in the stock and reduce the heat to low. Cook, covered, for 45 minutes, or until the stems of the greens are tender. The stock should reduce by half and the greens should be an autumnal color.

Add the chipotle chili and lemon zest. Season with smoked salt, stir, and serve.

½ cup (4½ oz/125 g) duck fat (see the Duck's Nuts recipe on page 62)

1 lb 2 oz (500 g) smoked bacon, diced

1 garlic bulb, peeled, cloves crushed

2 red chilies, finely chopped

2 brown onions, thinly sliced

2 teaspoons freshly ground black pepper

24–28 collard green leaves, stems removed, and coarsely chopped

¾ cup (7 fl oz/200 ml) apple cider vinegar (sweeter than regular vinegar)

8 cups (70 fl oz/2 liters) pork stock or chicken stock

2 canned chipotle chili pieces, finely chopped

zest of 1 lemon

smoked salt (see glossary), for seasoning

PICKLED GREEN TOMATOES

Plant one tomato plant and before you know it, it's *The Day of the Triffids*; they're taking over the entire garden, and you have no idea what to do with all their fruit. Pickle 'em, that's what you do. They'll be tart, fresh, and crunchy. Make sure you use unripe tomatoes for this recipe, not a green varietal, so the pickles are piquant. [Serves 6, with leftovers]

Cut each tomato into eight wedges. Transfer to a heatproof bowl, add the garlic, and set aside.

In a small, dry frying pan, toast the mustard seeds, peppercorns, and coriander seeds over medium heat for a few minutes, until fragrant.

Tip the spices into a saucepan. Add the vinegar, chili flakes, mace, salt, and sugar. Bring to a boil, then reduce the heat and simmer, uncovered, for 10 minutes. Pour the pickling liquid over the tomatoes, then immediately cover with a round of parchment paper.

Cool to room temperature, then transfer to a nonreactive container, preferably glass (plastic is okay, just make sure it's clean). Seal up and refrigerate for at least 1 week before using; stored in their brine, the pickled tomatoes will keep in the fridge for several months.

To plump up the mustard seeds, toast them in a hot, dry frying pan over medium–high heat for 1 minute, until they are smoking and fragrant. Add the sugar and 1½ cups (12 fl oz/375 ml) water, then cook over medium heat for 10 minutes, until the mixture is dry. Stir in the vinegar. The plumped mustard seeds will keep indefinitely in an airtight container in the fridge until required.

When ready to serve, strain the tomatoes from their pickling liquid, reserving the pickling liquid. Toss the tomatoes with the plumped mustard seeds, a splash of the pickling liquid, and a splash of your favorite extra virgin olive oil.

The pickled tomatoes are great on their own, or with fried chicken or poached seafood.

2 lb 4 oz (1 kg) garden-green tomatoes (unripe ones)
1 garlic bulb, papery skin on, cloves crushed
2 tablespoons black mustard seeds
1 tablespoon black peppercorns
1 tablespoon coriander seeds
4 cups (32 fl oz/1 liter) apple cider vinegar
2 teaspoons chili flakes
3 small whole mace pieces (do not use powdered mace, as it is too strongly flavored, and is too fine to strain from the pickling liquid)
¼ cup (1¾ oz/50 g) salt
1⅓ cups (9 oz/250 g) superfine sugar
extra virgin olive oil, for drizzling

PLUMPED MUSTARD SEEDS
3 tablespoons yellow mustard seeds
2 tablespoons sugar
½ teaspoon apple cider vinegar

FRIED GREEN TOMATOES

Make sure you use the real-deal cornmeal for crusting the tomatoes, not instant polenta. It has the perfect crunch to go with something creamy, like our USA Sauce (see page 199) or Remoulade (page 76). [Serves 6]

4 garden-green tomatoes (unripe ones, not a green varietal, so that they are tart)
1 cup (7 oz/200 g) lard
½ batch of Buttermilk Marinade (see "Marinating the Bird," page 23)
lemon cheeks, to serve

CORNMEAL MIX

1 cup (6¾ oz/190 g) stone-ground polenta (cornmeal); don't use instant polenta
2 tablespoons Old Bay Seasoning (see glossary)
2 teaspoons garlic powder
2 teaspoons onion powder
1 teaspoon freshly ground black pepper
1 teaspoon cayenne pepper
1 teaspoon celery seeds
1 cup (5½ oz/150 g) all-purpose flour

Core the tomatoes and cut them in half. Place them in a colander, season lightly with sea salt, then set aside in the sink for 30 minutes. Rinse the tomatoes and pat dry with a paper towel.

Heat the lard in a large frying pan over medium heat.

Meanwhile, place all the cornmeal mix ingredients in a mixing bowl and whisk until thoroughly combined.

Have the buttermilk marinade ready in another bowl.

Toss the tomatoes with the cornmeal mix, then dip each half into the marinade, coating the tomatoes all over. Repeat the process, then toss in the cornmeal mix a third and final time.

Immediately transfer all the tomatoes to the pan. Fry for 3–4 minutes on each side, or until the crust is a rich golden brown.

Drain on a paper towel. Season lightly with sea salt, freshly ground black pepper, and a squeeze of fresh lemon. Serve hot.

BUTTER LETTUCE & DANDELION SALAD with HOT BACON DRESSING

Butter lettuce is the easiest lettuce to grow. The leaves are beautifully soft and tender, just begging to be coated with a slick of warm bacon fat. [Serves 6]

To make the hot bacon dressing, put the pork fat in a saucepan and heat over medium–high heat until smoking. Add the bacon and cook for about 5 minutes, until the bacon is half crisp, darker in color, and the fat has released into the pan.

Add the garlic, chili flakes, and bay leaf. Toast for about 3 minutes, until the mixture smells really fragrant and the garlic starts to turn golden brown. Add the shallot and cook for about 4 minutes, until translucent.

Stir in the vinegar and sugar. Cook for 4–5 minutes over medium heat, scraping the bottom of the pan to release anything that's stuck. Season generously with sea salt and freshly ground black pepper.

Pour in the cream and bring to a boil, then remove from the heat. Add the thyme sprigs and leave to steep for 15 minutes, then remove and discard the thyme.

While the dressing is steeping, wash and thoroughly dry all the greens. Combine in a mixing bowl.

Add the lemon zest and lemon juice to the dressing, stirring to combine. Ladle the hot bacon dressing over the salad. The greens will slightly wilt, and the dressing will coat all the leaves. Haphazardly arrange the salad on a serving plate and enjoy straight away.

1 head of butter lettuce, core removed, leaves separated
1 bunch (5½ oz/150 g) dandelion greens, leaves separated, stems trimmed
1 bunch (1¾ oz/50 g) sorrel, small leaves only, stems trimmed
10–12 watercress sprigs

HOT BACON DRESSING
¼ cup (2¼ oz/60 g) pork fat (see Rendering Fat, page 245)
5½ oz (150 g) smoked bacon, diced
6 garlic cloves, crushed
2 teaspoons chili flakes
1 bay leaf
4 French shallots, diced
1 cup (8 fl oz/250 ml) champagne vinegar
2 teaspoons sugar
2 cups (17 fl oz/500 ml) whipping cream (35% fat)
4 thyme sprigs
zest and juice of 1 lemon

COLESLAW

Coleslaw should be rich and creamy. What you're looking for in a good slaw is the perfect wet/crunch factor. This one is it. [Serves 6]

¼ green cabbage
4 small brown pickling onions,
    peeled, topped, and tailed
1 large carrot, peeled
4 tablespoons chopped chives
½ batch of Old Bay Mayo
    (see page 204)

EQUIPMENT
Japanese mandoline

Cut the cabbage in half against the grain; using a mandoline, shred the cabbage lengthwise into ¹⁄₁₆ inch (2 mm) strands. Shave the onions into rings the same thickness as the cabbage.

Insert the julienne attachment into the mandoline, then shave the carrot diagonally.

In a bowl, toss the cabbage, onion, carrot, and chives by hand until evenly distributed. Just before serving, spoon in the mayo to suit your taste. Season with sea salt and freshly ground black pepper, and serve.

CORNCOBS with CHARRED CHILI DRESSING

When Naomi and I would walk home from work on a New York summer's night, the streets would be filled with food trucks and families cooking their fresh corn and homemade tortillas on little outdoor grills. This is my interpretation of their awesome-smelling street food. [Serves 6]

To make the buttermilk cheese, bring the buttermilk to a simmer in a small saucepan. Lightly whisk, just to break up the whey and the curds. Cook for 7–8 minutes, or until the liquid turns from cloudy white to more clear, and the curds are definitely separated from the whey.

Strain the mixture, discarding the whey; the mixture will appear white and lumpy. (If you're really clever, you can keep the whey and use it as a natural starter for pickles.)

Transfer the curds to a nonreactive container, season lightly with sea salt, then refrigerate for at least 1 hour, until hardened. The cheese will keep for up to 5 days in an airtight container in the fridge.

When you're ready to eat, fire up a barbecue to 480°F (250°C). Barbecue the corn and whole red chilies until the corn husks are black and charred, the corn kernels are cooked, and the chilies are black; this should take a good 20–25 minutes.

Finely chop the charred chilies and place in a bowl. Add the garlic, coriander, chili flakes, chipotle chili, pepper, butter, lime zest, lime juice, and corn chips. Toss to combine.

Peel back the corn husks. Dress the cobs with some of the chili dressing. Serve warm, topped with the grated buttermilk cheese, with the remaining charred chili dressing on the side.

4 corncobs, in their husks
4 long red chilies
4 garlic cloves, finely crushed
½ cup (1 oz/25 g) finely chopped cilantro stems and leaves
1 teaspoon chili flakes
1 canned chipotle chili, finely chopped
1 teaspoon freshly ground black pepper
⅔ cup (5½ oz/150 g) butter, melted
zest and juice of 1 lime
10 corn chips, crushed

BUTTERMILK CHEESE
2½ cups (20 fl oz/600 ml) buttermilk

BROAD BEANS on the BARBECUE

Every so often, I'm on the radio on Simon Marnie's weekend show. Simon thinks serving broad beans like this is about as lazy as a chef can get.

"You mean to tell me," he says, "that you char the beans in their casings, then whack 'em on a plate just like that, and the guest has to do all the work? Genius." [Serves 6]

2 lb 4 oz (1 kg) broad beans (about 30–40 pods), rinsed and dried, cleaned of all dirt
large grains or flakes of sea salt
2 tablespoons extra virgin olive oil
Lemon Jam (see page 198), to serve
Romesco Sauce (see page 198), to serve

EQUIPMENT
hooded barbecue

Heat a hooded barbecue to 480°F (250°C).

Lay the broad beans across a clean barbecue grill plate (this is preferable to a wire rack) and close the lid. Char the outside of the husk, flipping the beans after about 2 minutes, then cook for an additional 2 minutes with the lid closed. You'll know when the beans are done as the moisture will escape, leaving the pod lightly puffed; touching the pod, the bean should still be firm, but not mushy. (Or you could always peel one open and taste it!)

Remove the beans from the barbecue and place in a large bowl. Season with sea salt, drizzle with the olive oil, and toss to coat.

Spread the beans on a platter. Serve with Lemon Jam and Romesco Sauce. The best part about this dish is that you eat the beans with your hands. Tear open the pod, dip in the Lemon Jam first, then the Romesco, and munch away.

ROASTED BROCCOLI with LEMON JAM, WALNUT BUTTER & AGED GOUDA

This broccoli dish is a consistent favorite on the Hartsyard menu. You can also use the tangy, lemony Walnut Butter to accompany fish.

Don't be intimidated by the use of anchovy juice as a seasoning here. It doesn't add a fishy quality, more a different sort of briny salt flavor, which pairs beautifully with the broccoli. Our local supermarket actually stocks anchovy juice, but if you have trouble tracking it down, good-quality fish sauce will suffice. [Serves 6]

4 heads of broccoli

⅓ cup (2½ fl oz/80 ml) whipping cream (35% fat)

grapeseed oil, or another oil or fat of your choice, for frying

2 tablespoons anchovy juice, or good-quality fish sauce

Lemon Jam (see page 198), to serve

⅓ cup (2½ fl oz/80 ml) mustard oil (from Indian supermarkets and specialty stores)

¾ cup (3½ oz/100 g) aged Gouda cheese, shaved

WALNUT BUTTER

1 cup (3½ oz/100 g) butter

1¼ cups (9 oz/250 g) walnuts

1 lemon, zested, then peeled and cut into segments, removing the membranes

2 tablespoons champagne vinegar

Pour 16 cups (140 fl oz/4 liters) water into a large saucepan. Season with sea salt, making it taste like the ocean, then bring to a boil.

Cut all the broccoli heads into stalks and florets. Reserve the stalks. Set the larger florets aside; put the smaller ones in a bowl, as we'll use these to make a broccoli purée.

Using a vegetable peeler, trim half the reserved broccoli stalks, peeling until you reach the heart of the stem. Keep all the trimmings in the bowl with the small florets. Set the trimmed broccoli stalks aside; they'll be used to dress the finished dish.

Take the remaining broccoli stalks and slice them as thinly as possible. Add them to the smaller florets and trimmings in the bowl. Now tip the contents of the entire bowl into the pan of boiling water and blanch for 4–5 minutes, or until soft. You want all the broccoli bits to be soft enough to purée, yet still retain a nice green color.

Immediately scoop the broccoli into a blender. Pour in the cream and purée for 4–5 minutes, until completely smooth. Chill immediately; your purée is done!

Cut the remaining raw broccoli stalks into slices about ⅛ inch (3 mm) thick. Set aside.

To make the Walnut Butter, combine the butter and walnuts in a saucepan and cook over low heat for about 5 minutes, until the walnuts become aromatic and the butter starts to brown. The butter and walnuts should be browning and toasting at the same rate; the milk solids in the butter should turn no darker than the color of the walnut skins, as any further cooking will make the butter taste burnt and bitter. Remove from the heat and leave to cool at room temperature.

When cooled, crush the walnuts in the butter until a rough paste forms. (You could use a large spoon for this, a mortar and pestle, or pulse them together in a food processor.)

Season with the lemon zest, vinegar, and a good grind of black pepper. Fold the lemon segments through.

TO FINISH
Heat a cast-iron frying pan until very hot. Add enough grapeseed oil to coat the entire bottom of the pan. Lay the reserved large broccoli florets in the hot pan, flattest side down, to ensure the maximum surface area will be cooked.

Cook the broccoli florets on the one side until a really nice, golden crust develops, and the broccoli smells roasted and aromatic. Be patient, as this makes it taste like magic; it will take about 5–6 minutes altogether. In the last minute of cooking, flip the broccoli florets over and sizzle the other side.

Place the roasted broccoli in a bowl and season with the anchovy juice.

Smear some lemon jam across a serving plate, along with the Walnut Butter and dollops of the broccoli purée.

Place the roasted broccoli florets on top, then the shaved raw broccoli stalks. Finish with the mustard oil and shaved Gouda…and prepare to be amazed.

BRAISED OKRA & TOMATOES

Basically, okra is only good if it's pickled, fried, or braised. Then the slippery little buggers become very good indeed. [Serves 6]

In a 4-quart (140 fl oz/4 liter) stockpot, melt the bacon fat. Sweat the garlic over medium–high heat for 3 minutes, or until golden. Add the onion and cook for 7–8 minutes, until translucent.

Add the chopped chili, chili flakes, thyme, bay leaf, and mustard seeds. Cook for an additional 5 minutes, then stir in the vinegar and tomatoes, and cook for another 5 minutes.

Now add the okra and stock. Simmer over medium heat for about 35 minutes—the liquid should be reduced by half; the mixture should have a stewlike consistency, and should stick to a spoon nicely.

Add the sea salt and hot sauce to taste. Serve hot.

⅓ cup (2¾ oz/80 g) bacon fat (see Rendering Fat, page 244)
1 garlic bulb, peeled and sliced (not too thinly)
2 brown onions, diced
1 long red chili, charred on a very hot barbecue or chargrill pan, then chopped
2 teaspoons chili flakes
1 tablespoon chopped thyme leaves
1 bay leaf
1 teaspoon yellow mustard seeds
¼ cup (2 fl oz/60 ml) white balsamic vinegar (see glossary)
1 can (14 oz/400 g) diced tomatoes
1 lb 2 oz (500 g) okra, stems removed, sliced in half
2 cups (17 fl oz/500 ml) chicken stock (store-bought is fine)
2 teaspoons sea salt
Hartsyard Hot Sauce (see page 188), to taste

RAW ARTICHOKE & MUSHROOM SALAD

This dish is a bit of a shout-out to my friend Steve Santoro, who was originally one of my teachers. We later opened a restaurant together in Connecticut, and it was Steve who brought me back from Puerto Rico to New York City, to work alongside him at a restaurant where there was a tall, redheaded Australian hostess whom I wanted to date from the first moment I laid eyes on her. So I guess you could call Steve a matchmaker of sorts. I also call him the King of Vegetables. [Serves 4]

BLACK TRUFFLE OIL

1⅓ cups (3½ oz/100 g) button mushrooms
3½ tablespoons (1½ fl oz/50 ml) black truffle oil
½ teaspoon sea salt
2 teaspoons soy sauce

EQUIPMENT
food dehydrator

Using a food processor, blitz the mushrooms into a paste of uniform consistency.

Spread the mushroom paste over a dehydrator tray. Dry on high for 24 hours, or until the mushroom is black, dry, and crispy.

Transfer to a blender and add the truffle oil, salt, and soy sauce. Blend until smooth and silky, letting the blender run for 4–5 minutes.

You'll only need half the truffle oil for this salad. The remainder will keep indefinitely in an airtight jar for next time.

LEMON, GARLIC & CHILI VINAIGRETTE

2 tablespoons Lemon Jam (see page 198)
1 tablespoon Dijon mustard
2 teaspoons chili flakes
¼ batch of Garlic Confit (see page 203)
½ cup (4 fl oz/125 ml) white wine vinegar
2 cups (17 fl oz/500 ml) canola oil

In a food processor or blender, blitz the Lemon Jam, mustard, chili flakes, garlic confit, vinegar, and ½ cup (4 fl oz/125 ml) water until smooth; this usually takes about 1 minute.

With the motor running, slowly add the canola oil and emulsify until the mixture is homogeneous and coats the back of a spoon. If the vinaigrette is too thick and viscous, slowly work in another ¼ cup (2 fl oz/60 ml) of water.

You'll only need half the vinaigrette for this salad. The remainder will keep in an airtight container in the fridge for several weeks.

PARMESAN CHIPS

½ cup (3½ oz/100 g) Parmigiano Reggiano cheese

Preheat the oven to 350°F (180°C). Line a baking tray with parchment paper, grate the cheese on top, then season liberally with freshly ground black pepper.

Bake until golden brown and bubbling, about 9–10 minutes.

Remove from the oven, let cool, then break into shards. The chips will keep in an airtight container in the pantry for 3–4 days.

PARMESAN CUSTARD

4 egg yolks
2½ cups (20 fl oz/600 ml) whipping cream (35% fat)
½ teaspoon freshly grated nutmeg
2 cups (9 oz/250 g) Grana Padano cheese, grated

EQUIPMENT
sugar thermometer

In the top of a double boiler or a heatproof bowl set above a saucepan of simmering water, combine the egg yolks, cream, and nutmeg. Gently bring the mixture to 172°F (78°C). Add the cheese and cook for about 5 minutes, until the cheese starts to melt.

Transfer to a blender or food processor and purée until smooth; the custard will not be lumpy, but there will be granules, so strain it through a fine mesh sieve into a container.

Refrigerate for at least 2 hours, until set.

You'll only need half the custard for this salad, but that's okay—the leftover custard will keep in the fridge for 2–3 days, and is also delicious served hot with steamed bitter broccoli and kale, or spread on crusty bread.

FOR THE SALAD

2 teaspoons citric acid
2 globe artichokes
2 Jerusalem artichokes, washed thoroughly
7 oz (200 g) A-grade button mushrooms
4 celery stalks, plus 18–20 celery leaves (light green bits only), to garnish
canola oil, for deep-frying
6–7 kale or cavolo nero leaves, stems removed
½ cup (3½ oz/100 g) Grana Padano cheese, shaved

EQUIPMENT
Japanese mandoline
sugar thermometer

In a bowl, dissolve the citric acid in 4 cups (32 fl oz/1 liter) of water. Individually remove the outer leaves of the globe artichokes. Cut the top off each artichoke, then pare away the outer, fibrous layer. Submerge the artichoke hearts in the citric acid solution, to keep them from discoloring.

Using a mandoline, slice the Jerusalem artichokes to a ¹⁄₁₆ inch (2 mm) thickness. Place in cold water (to remove the starch and to keep them from browning) until ready to cook.

Using the mandoline, thinly slice the mushrooms and set aside. Shave the celery and set aside separately.

Heat about 2 inches (5 cm) of canola oil in a deep fryer or heavy-based saucepan to 285°F (140°C) (if using a saucepan, check the temperature using a sugar thermometer).

Remove the Jerusalem artichoke chips from their water bath and pat dry. Deep-fry until golden brown and crisp (about 4–5 minutes). Drain on a paper towel and season with sea salt.

Increase the oil temperature to 315°F (160°C). Be careful, as the oil will spit (use a splatter guard). Deep fry the kale for about 40 seconds, or until bright green and crisp. Drain on a paper towel and season with sea salt.

Remove the globe artichoke hearts from their citric acid solution and pat dry. Slice immediately on a mandoline, to a thickness of ¹⁄₁₆ inch (2 mm). Place in a mixing bowl along with the mushrooms, shaved celery, and shaved cheese. Drizzle with half the lemon, garlic, and chili vinaigrette; season with sea salt and freshly ground black pepper; and toss gently.

TO ASSEMBLE

Divide half the Parmesan Custard among four serving plates. Scatter the salad over the plates.

Garnish with the celery leaves, the fried kale, and Jerusalem artichoke chips. Top with all the Parmesan Chips. Drizzle half the truffle oil over and serve immediately.

ICEBERG LETTUCE, TOMATO & GRAINS

Iceberg is the unsung hero of lettuces. Here it is celebrated in its own right. Crispy grains, puffed rice, eggs: this dish is almost healthy. [Serves 6]

¼ cup (1¾ oz/50 g) mixed (white, black and red) quinoa
juice of ½ lemon
dash of olive oil
1½ cups (1½ oz/45 g) watercress sprigs
4 kale leaves, stems removed
1 head of iceberg lettuce
1 cup (8 fl oz/250 ml) Green Goddess Dressing (see page 203)
2 soft-poached eggs, or soft-boiled eggs (peeled and cut in half)
dill sprigs, to garnish

OVEN-DRIED TOMATOES
4 extremely ripe roma tomatoes, cored and cut in half lengthwise
1 tablespoon olive oil
½ teaspoon freshly ground black pepper
1 teaspoon coarse sea salt
1 teaspoon superfine sugar
2 thyme sprigs, leaves picked
1 garlic clove, crushed

SHERRY VINAIGRETTE
1½ tablespoons sherry vinegar
2 teaspoons honey
2 teaspoons mustard
1½ tablespoons canola oil
1½ tablespoons extra virgin olive oil
½ teaspoon sea salt
½ teaspoon sugar

PUFFED WILD RICE
1 cup (8 fl oz/250 ml) canola or vegetable oil
¼ cup (1¾ oz/50 g) wild rice

To oven-dry the tomatoes, preheat the oven to 225°F (110°C). Line a baking tray with parchment paper. Combine all the ingredients in a bowl, tossing to coat the tomatoes. Lay them on the baking tray, cut side up, and bake for 6–8 hours (or overnight), until the tomatoes have shrunk to half their size, and look shriveled but not dry. (They will keep in an airtight container in the fridge for up to 1 week.)

To make the vinaigrette, combine the vinegar, honey, and mustard, and whisk thoroughly. Slowly whisk in the oils to emulsify them. Stir in the sea salt and sugar and set aside.

Cook the quinoa according to the package instructions. Add the lemon juice and olive oil, toss, then set aside while finishing the salad.

To puff the rice, heat the canola oil in a frying pan over high heat, until smoking. Add the rice; it will immediately puff. Slowly shake the pan for about 10 seconds—the rice will look tan and cracked. Immediately strain into a metal container, reserving the oil for another use. Season the puffed rice lightly with sea salt.

In a mixing bowl, dress the watercress and kale with about ¼ cup (2 fl oz/60 ml) of the vinaigrette (any leftover vinaigrette will keep indefinitely in an airtight jar in the fridge).

Trim the lettuce and cut in thirds horizontally. Dress the middle disk with most of the Green Goddess Dressing. (Use the remaining lettuce disks in another salad or on sandwiches.)

Arrange the lettuce on a plate. Scatter with the quinoa, tomatoes, watercress, kale, and puffed rice. Top with the eggs, drizzle with the remaining dressing, garnish with dill, and serve.

HARTSYARD HOT SAUCE
DIRTY CHICKEN GRAVY
ROASTED VEGETABLE BARBECUE SAUCE
WHITE SAUSAGE GRAVY
SUNGA'S WHITE KIMCHI
LEMON JAM
ROMESCO SAUCE
RUSSIAN DRESSING
USA SAUCE
SMOKED MAPLE SYRUP
GREEN GODDESS DRESSING
GARLIC CONFIT
OLD BAY MAYO
DRY RANCH SPICE
MUSTARD BARBECUE SAUCE
TOGARASHI SALT

SAUCES

A SCENT BY HARTSYARD

When I went into labor with our firstborn, I was bent over the couch in our living room, dressed in nothing but my undies and sort of moaning a half-song while Gregory rubbed my lower back.

Suddenly, the door to our apartment swung open and our downstairs neighbor walked in carrying a pot. "I just made some borscht," she announced. "I thought you might like some."

"Margie," said Gregory in disbelief, "Nome is in labor."

"Oh, right. I wondered what that was. I thought you were just having really loud sex." She walked past us and into the kitchen. "I'll just put this in the fridge then, shall I? You're probably a bit busy for it now. Don't worry though, you're meant to eat it cold."

I continued to moan through what was quickly becoming a very short, very intense labor.

"Well," she said, as she walked back through, "good luck then. I guess we'll see you when you get home," and she closed the door behind her.

We had only recently moved back to Australia and were living upstairs in the house of a family friend, a tiny but fabulous place with a view of both Sydney Harbour Bridge and the Anzac Bridge, and so long as you didn't mind the downstairs dwellers wandering in whenever they liked, it was the nicest place I'd ever lived. It wasn't a deliberate open-door policy, but we shared a common front door and often a drink on the balcony while the sun set over the bridges, so the line, along with our vision, slowly got blurred.

Fast forward twelve months and the baby in that labor story was now the one-year-old daughter we were sharing the bedroom with, while both of us were unemployed and plotting the opening of our first restaurant. Each night I would breast-feed with one arm and do computer work with the other, while Gregory would recipe-test in our thoroughly inadequate home kitchen, going through eleven different chilies before settling on the ones for the hot sauce, mucking around with batters for the different breads and English muffins, experimenting with marinades for the lamb ribs, and dehydrating masses and masses of fennel pollen. Every night while we worked, the dehydrator would whirr away in the corner, filling the small apartment with a rich sweetness that frustrated bees during the day as they

buzzed at the screen door, knowing there was something attractive inside, if only they could get in and find it.

Now, every time I smell fennel in the Hartsyard kitchen, I'm immediately transported back to that crazy, exhausting, exhilarating time. No sleep, no money, no time, no clue; Ash, our friend (and restaurant designer), flying in from New York and sleeping on the living room floor; Mount Washmore growing in the corner as we washed but never folded our clothes; endless trips to hardware stores and countless emails to the Liquor Licensing Board; paint samples stacked in the corner, wineglasses on top of those—a leaning tower of hope and risk. Late, late nights, pre-dawn mornings; the supplies in the pantry running ever lower as the savings dwindled and we had less and less money to spend on food. A baby, it seems, cannot survive on breast milk and dried fennel pollen alone.

No matter. She had no clue, and neither did we, forging ahead, learning more about people and business and money and luck and making your own luck, and still more about people than we had previously learned in the rest of our entire lives combined. As one brother kept saying to me, "You won't learn this in an MBA."

I'd taken a step like this once before, when I packed my bags and moved to New York with not much more than a strong sense of purpose, and that had turned out all right. We just needed to stop every now and then and remember to smell the fennel.

Eau de Fenouil: A Scent by Hartsyard. Intense, passionate, fresh, consuming, spicy, layered, and new.

HARTSYARD HOT SAUCE

"That's all it is?" asked Naomi, when she read the ingredients list for this sauce. "With all the compliments it gets, I half-expected it to contain essence of unicorn."

Without trying to sound conceited, this is the item on the Hartsyard menu that receives the most praise. [Makes about 8 cups/70 fl oz/2 liters]

---

7 oz (200 g) long red fresno chilies (see glossary)

7 oz (200 g) brown onions, halved

4 cups (32 fl oz/1 liter) white vinegar

⅓ cup (3½ oz/100 g) sea salt

generous ½ cup (3½ oz/100 g) garlic cloves

7 tablespoons (3½ oz/100 g) unsalted butter

EQUIPMENT

hooded barbecue

9 oz (250 g) oak food-grade woodchips (never use chunks or pellets)

cast-iron pan (not enamel-coated)

On a barbecue with a lid, lay out half the chilies and half the onions, leaving enough space to house a black cast-iron pan. Place the empty cast-iron pan on the stovetop until ridiculously hot (roughly 5 minutes on full heat).

Meanwhile, in a 3-quart (105 fl oz/3 liter) stockpot, combine the remaining chilies and onions, the vinegar, sea salt, and garlic. Bring to a slow simmer, never allowing the mixture to boil.

When the cast-iron pan is at smelting temperature, cover the bottom with at least ½ inch (1 cm) of oak chips. Leave until the chips start to smolder and smoke (almost instantaneous)—they should never ignite.

Move the cast-iron pan to the barbecue very carefully, then close the barbecue lid and leave to smoke. If the chips are still smoking after a minimum of 20 minutes, let them go until they're finished; but if they're done, place the whole smoked vegetables in the simmering stockpot (which by now should have been bubbling away for 30 minutes).

Simmer for an additional 30 minutes, ensuring the mixture never boils. After 1 hour of total cooking, remove the stockpot from the heat.

Stir in the butter, cover, and wait until the pot is cool to the touch, then wrap the top of the container with plastic wrap to form a seal. Leave at room temperature for 48 hours.

After 2 days, blend all the ingredients until they're smooth enough to strain through a colander. This should remove large chunks, leaving behind a fine pulp.

Transfer to sterile bottles or airtight containers and refrigerate until required; the sauce will easily keep for a week or two.

DIRTY CHICKEN GRAVY

Dirty like the color of mud, and delicious like the greatest gravy you've ever tasted, this sensational sauce has a super-chickeny flavor and just begs to be served with Mashed Potatoes (see page 131). [Serves 6]

Preheat the oven to 345°F (175°C).

Chop each chicken carcass into four or five bits. Set half the chicken bones aside. Set half the garlic, carrot, onion, and celery aside.

Put the remaining chicken bones in a large roasting pan with the remaining garlic, carrot, onion, and celery. Roast for about 1¼ hours, or until the chicken bones are a deep, rich brown color.

Remove from the oven, then transfer the roasted bones, vegetables, and all the fat from the roasting pan into a stockpot. Add the stock, half the thyme, and half the bay leaves. Bring to a simmer, then cook, uncovered, over low heat for 2 hours, periodically skimming the impurities from the top. Strain, discarding the solids.

Meanwhile, roast the reserved chicken bones and reserved vegetables, repeating the process as before. Remove from the oven, then transfer the roasted bones, vegetables, and all the fat into another medium-sized stockpot. Add the strained cooking liquid from the previous stock, and the remaining thyme and bay leaves. Simmer, uncovered, over low heat for an additional 2 hours, periodically skimming the impurities from the top. This is your gravy.

When the gravy is nearly ready, make your roux. Melt the animal fat in a small saucepan. Whisk in the flour, then cook over low heat until the flour starts to turn golden brown, about 15 minutes. Now cook for an additional 5 minutes; the flour will start to become fragrant.

Strain the gravy into a smaller stockpot, discarding the solids. Add the roux to the gravy (it will bind the fats and liquids in the gravy). Cook over medium heat until reduced by half, or to about 2 cups (17 fl oz/500 ml). The mixture should be a rich brown color and will thicken as it boils; it should easily coat the back of a spoon.

Strain into a bowl, then season with lots of freshly ground black pepper, a squeeze of lemon juice, and the hot sauce. Slowly whisk in the chicken fat, and you're ready to serve.

6 chicken carcasses
2 garlic bulbs, halved (no need to peel them for this recipe)
2 carrots, halved
4 brown onions, halved
2 celery stalks, chopped
8 cups (70 fl oz/2 liters) reduced-salt chicken stock
12 thyme sprigs
4 bay leaves
lemon juice, to taste
2 dashes of Hartsyard Hot Sauce (see page 188)
¼ cup (2¼ oz/60 g) roasted chicken fat, melted

ROUX
½ cup (4½ oz/125 g) of your favorite animal fat (see Rendering Fat, pages 244–245); because it's a dirty gravy, anything goes!
½ cup (2½ oz/75 g) all-purpose flour

ROASTED VEGETABLE BARBECUE SAUCE

At the restaurant we smoke our vegetables for this sauce, but I tried to come up with a more user-friendly method. This is all things good about smoking without the effort—caramelly, roasted, sweet, and a little bit sour. It is excellent with fish, beef, pork, or chicken...or out of the fridge on a spoon. [Makes about 4 cups/32 fl oz/1 liter]

1 red pepper

1 green pepper

2 brown onions, quartered

1 carrot, cut lengthwise and quartered

2 garlic bulbs, kept whole, still in their papery skins, crushed

olive oil, for coating

1 cinnamon stick

1 star anise

1 tablespoon coriander seeds

1 tablespoon cumin seeds

4 long red chilies, stems removed

1 can (14 oz/400 g) whole, peeled tomatoes

¾ cup (7 fl oz/200 ml) maple syrup

¾ cup (7 fl oz/200 ml) balsamic vinegar

¾ cup (7 fl oz/200 ml) Worcestershire sauce

3½ tablespoons (1½ fl oz/50 ml) liquid smoke (available from specialty stores)

1 rosemary sprig

5 thyme sprigs

1 bay leaf

½ cup (3¼ oz/95 g) dark brown sugar

Preheat the oven to 290°F (145°C). Cut the peppers in half and discard the stems, membranes, and seeds. Place in a bowl with the onion, carrot, and garlic. Toss with olive oil to coat, then lay out on a baking tray. Bake for 2½ hours, turning every 30 minutes, until the vegetables are roasted, softened, and syrupy.

Meanwhile, toast the cinnamon stick, star anise, coriander seeds, and cumin seeds in a small, dry frying pan over medium heat for a few minutes, until fragrant. Tip the spices into an 8-quart (280 fl oz/8 liter) stockpot, add the remaining ingredients, and bring to a boil. Reduce the heat and simmer, uncovered, for about 2½ hours, while the vegetables are roasting.

Stir the roasted vegetables into the sauce. Simmer over low heat for an additional 2½ hours. Allow to cool to room temperature.

Remove the cinnamon stick and star anise, then blend the mixture in batches until smooth. Strain through a fine mesh sieve. Transfer to sterile bottles or airtight containers and refrigerate until required; the sauce will keep for a week or two.

WHITE SAUSAGE GRAVY

The key to this gravy is toasting the garlic until you can't toast it any more. Also don't try to be healthy—make sure you use all the fat from the sausage, for maximum flavor. We serve this one with our fried chicken and Buttermilk Biscuits (see page 139). [Serves 6]

Heat the chicken fat and butter in a 4-quart (140 fl oz/4-liter) stockpot until warm. Add the garlic and toast over medium heat until golden brown delicious. Add the onion and cook for about 8 minutes, or until translucent.

Add the pork, breaking it into a granulated texture using a wooden spoon or a whisk. Continue cooking and stirring for about 5 minutes, or until cooked through. Stir in the flour, chili flakes, pepper, and sea salt to taste, then cook for another 5 minutes, or until the mixture is thoroughly combined and no lumps exist.

Add the milk and cream simultaneously, stirring constantly with a wooden spoon until the mixture boils. It's tricky because it's a thick mixture when it cooks, so be careful of scorching. If the sauce is too thick, add a little more milk once the mixture comes to a boil.

Adjust the temperature to a low bubbling simmer and cook for another 30 minutes. Your gravy is now ready to eat! Please test with the biggest spoon possible and get ready to burn the roof of your mouth.

1 cup (8 oz/250 g) chicken fat (see Rendering Fat, page 244)

7 tablespoons (3½ oz/100 g) unsalted butter

1 garlic bulb, peeled and very thinly sliced using a microplane

1 brown onion, finely diced

1 lb 2 oz (500 g) pork sausage mince (from your butcher); if you can't get this, buy pork sausages and remove the casings

½ cup (2½ oz/75 g) all-purpose flour

2 teaspoons chili flakes

2 teaspoons coarsely ground black pepper

4 cups (32 fl oz/1 liter) milk

1½ cups (14 fl oz/400 ml) whipping cream (35% fat)

SUNGA'S WHITE KIMCHI

Red kimchi is typically spicier than this version, which is more savory. It's fermented a bit longer and has a nice effervescence on the tongue. [Serves 6]

1 Chinese cabbage (wong bok)
sea salt, for sprinkling
7 oz (200 g) Chinese radish
    (see glossary), diced
1 long red chili, stem removed,
    then chopped
1 long green chili, stem removed,
    then chopped
3 scallions, chopped
4 x 8 inch (10 x 20 cm) piece of
    kombu seaweed
¼ cup (1½ oz/45 g) rice flour
½ brown onion, roughly chopped
8 garlic cloves, peeled
1 oz (30 g) fresh ginger, peeled
    and roughly chopped

Cut the cabbage lengthwise into quarters, then into thick wedges. Open the leaves out, leaving them joined together at the core. Sprinkle generously with sea salt and leave to sit for 4 hours.

Give the cabbage a quick rinse to wash off the excess salt. Squeeze dry and place the wedges in a clean plastic container, layering them with the radish, chili, and scallions.

In a saucepan, bring the kombu and 8 cups (70 fl oz/ 2 liters) of water to a simmer. Leave to simmer, uncovered, for 30 minutes. Strain the liquid, discarding the kombu.

Add the rice flour to the warm liquid, then whisk for 2 minutes until it thickens. Remove from the heat and refrigerate the liquid until cooled to room temperature (you don't want it to cook the cabbage in the next step).

Using a food processor, blend the onion, garlic, and ginger together, until the mixture almost becomes a juice. Add to the cooled liquid, then season to taste with sea salt. Pour the mixture over the vegetables.

Cover the surface with parchment paper, pushing down to submerge the vegetables. Seal and refrigerate for 1 week before using; the kimchi will keep for 1 month.

LEMON JAM

When planning the Broad Beans dish on page 172, I knew it had to include lemons. Squeezing lemon juice over or serving with charred lemon slices would have been okay, but I wanted something you could dip the beans into, that would stick to your fingers and make you lick them.
[Makes about 2 cups/16 oz/400 g]

thinly peeled rind of 2 lemons
¾ cup (5½ oz/160 g) superfine sugar
½ teaspoon agar-agar powder (a gelling agent, available from Asian grocers)

Combine the lemon rind, sugar, and 1 cup (8 fl oz/250 ml) of water in a saucepan. Stir over medium heat until the sugar has dissolved. Bring to a boil, then reduce the heat to low and simmer for 1 hour, to allow the flavors to develop and the liquid to reduce slightly. Set aside to cool.

Add the agar-agar and stir to combine, then increase the heat and boil for 1 minute. Pour into a large container and refrigerate until set (about 3–4 hours).

Process the jam in a blender until smooth. The jam can be refrigerated in an airtight container for up to 2 days.

ROMESCO SAUCE

Sweet and sour roasted goodness... [Makes about 4 cups/32 fl oz/1 liter]

6 roma tomatoes
2 large red peppers, halved, seeds and membranes removed
generous ½ cup (5 fl oz/150 ml) extra virgin olive oil
3 slices sourdough bread, about 3½ oz (100 g), roughly torn
1 red onion, quartered
1 garlic bulb, separated into cloves, but left unpeeled
⅔ cup (3½ oz/100 g) almonds
⅓ cup (1¾ oz/50 g) hazelnuts
7 tablespoons (3½ fl oz/100 ml) sherry vinegar
1 teaspoon smoked paprika

Preheat the oven to 350°F (180°C). Line two baking trays with parchment paper.

In a large bowl, combine all the ingredients except the vinegar and paprika. Season with sea salt and freshly ground black pepper, and toss to combine. Spread out on the baking trays and roast, turning occasionally, for 45–55 minutes, until the onion is golden and tender.

When cool enough to handle, squeeze the garlic cloves out of their skins, into a food processor. Add the other roasted ingredients, and process until the mixture is well combined to your desired consistency.

Add the vinegar and paprika, then pulse again to a coarse paste. Season to taste. The romesco can be refrigerated in an airtight container for up to 2 weeks.

FRIED CHICKEN & FRIENDS

RUSSIAN DRESSING

The only thing that makes corned beef or pastrami and sauerkraut on rye taste any better than it already does is this dressing. You'll need to pickle the onion for 24 hours, so begin a day ahead. [Makes about 2 cups/16 fl oz/400 ml]

Simmer the vinegar and sugar in a small saucepan until the sugar has dissolved. Put the onion in a heatproof container, pour the pickling liquid over, then cover and refrigerate for 24 hours.

Drain the pickled onion, reserving the pickling liquid. Combine with the remaining ingredients. Season to taste with sea salt and freshly ground black pepper, adding enough reserved pickling liquid to achieve a sour flavor.

The dressing will keep in an airtight container in the fridge for up to 1 week.

½ cup (4 fl oz/125 ml) white vinegar
½ cup (3¾ oz/110 g) sugar
1 small white onion, very finely chopped
1 cup (8 oz/250 g) mayonnaise
½ cup (4 fl oz/125 ml) ketchup
1 dill pickle (see page 37), diced
½ cup (1 oz/30 g) chopped dill
2 dashes of Tabasco sauce

USA SAUCE

Sunga, our former sous chef, came up with this name. He said it's because I made it up and I'm from the USA. Fair enough, although you might also know this as buttermilk ranch dressing. It's important to make this one the day before serving, so the cultures in the sour cream set it into a denser dressing. [Makes about 2 cups/17 fl oz/500 ml]

Mix all the ingredients in a mixing bowl until thoroughly combined. Season liberally with sea salt and freshly ground black pepper. This dressing will keep in an airtight container in the fridge for up to 1 week.

1 cup (8 oz/250 g) mayonnaise
1 cup (8 oz/250 g) sour cream
¼ cup (1¾ oz/50 g) onion powder
2 tablespoons garlic powder
¼ cup (2 fl oz/60 ml) Worcestershire sauce
juice of 2 lemons
1 tablespoon Dry Ranch Spice (see page 204)

LEMON JAM

RUSSIAN DRESSING

USA SAUCE

MUSTARD BARBECUE SAUCE

ROMESCO SAUCE

GREEN
GODDESS
DRESSING

SMOKED
MAPLE
SYRUP

OLD
BAY
MAYO

SMOKED MAPLE SYRUP

There was a property near where I grew up in Johnson, New York, that I went to once with my dad. Being the middle child of seven kids, one-on-one occasions like that were rare. I also remember it because it was the first (and only) time I'd sourced my own maple syrup. Or maybe it sticks in my mind because it was the first time I got stitches, when another kid covered a rock with snow and pegged it at my head during a snowball fight.

We'd tapped the swelling trees the day before, so we'd returned to fill a 300-gallon drum with maple water that we then placed on top of a fire and left to simmer away until all that was left was the rich, thick syrup. This can take hours, even days, which is why we were having a snowball fight.

I know a lot of you won't bother or may not be able to smoke your maple syrup, but whatever you do, please use the real deal. Don't buy imitation maple syrup because it's cheaper. It's cheap because it's fake.

This syrup is brilliant with fried chicken, and drizzled over Waffles (see page 140) and vanilla ice cream. [Makes about 4 cups/32 fl oz/1 liter]

---

4 cups (32 fl oz/1 liter) Canadian
   maple syrup

EQUIPMENT
9 oz (250 g) oak food-grade
   woodchips (never use
   chunks or pellets)
hooded barbecue
enamel baking dish
cast-iron pan (not enamel-coated)

Pour the maple syrup into an enamel baking dish (not a metal one because it will contort). Place the baking dish on a barbecue that has a lid, leaving enough space to house a black cast-iron pan.

Place the empty cast-iron pan on the stovetop until ridiculously hot (roughly 5 minutes on full heat).

When the cast-iron pan is at smelting temperature, cover the bottom with at least ½ inch (1 cm) of oak chips. Leave until the chips start to smolder and smoke (almost instantaneous)—they should never ignite.

Move the cast-iron pan to the barbecue very carefully, then close the barbecue lid and leave to smoke. If the chips are still smoking after a minimum of 20 minutes, let them go until they're finished.

Pour the smoked syrup into a sterile jar and seal well. The syrup will keep indefinitely in a cool dark place.

GREEN GODDESS DRESSING

Pour this bright, creamy, delicious dressing over lettuce and change reluctant lettuce-eaters' hearts. The star of our salad on page 182, it is also ridiculously good with vegetable crudités. [Makes 4 cups/32 fl oz/1 liter]

In a blender, process the sour cream, watercress, capers, and garlic confit until smooth.

Transfer to a mixing bowl and taste for salt (capers can be very salty). Fold in the herbs and lemon juice and season liberally with freshly ground black pepper. Taste again for salt and adjust as needed. Stir in the buttermilk; the consistency should be similar to ketchup.

Refrigerate in an airtight container until needed. The dressing will keep for up to 3 days.

1 cup (8 oz/250 g) sour cream
scant ¾ cup (4½ oz/125 g) watercress, large stems removed
2 tablespoons small capers, drained and rinsed of brine
¼ batch of Garlic Confit (see below)
½ cup (1 oz/25 g) thinly sliced chives
3 tablespoons thinly sliced tarragon (*not* chopped, as this will bruise the leaves)
½ cup (1 oz/30 g) thinly sliced dill
3 tablespoons thinly sliced flat-leaf (Italian) parsley
juice of 2 lemons
generous ¾ cup (7 fl oz/200 ml) buttermilk

GARLIC CONFIT

With its mellow flavor, this pops up in quite a few of our recipes. It's worth making more than you need; you can spread any leftovers on toast, or use in vinaigrettes, marinades, stews, and soups. [Makes 4 bulbs]

Put the garlic in a small saucepan, season with sea salt and freshly ground black pepper, and cover with the olive oil. Simmer very slowly on the lowest heat for about 1 hour, or until the garlic becomes sweet, tan in color, and quite soft, but still retains its shape.

Stored in the oil, the garlic confit will keep in an airtight container in the fridge for several weeks.

4 garlic bulbs, separated into individual cloves, then peeled
2 cups (17 fl oz/500 ml) extra virgin olive oil

OLD BAY MAYO

This is one of the first things I thought of when we opened Hartsyard. Mayonnaise and Old Bay Seasoning together are a pretty heavenly combo. The only thing that makes it better is the miso. [Makes 1 lb 9 oz/700 g]

2 egg yolks (save the whites for our Aperol Sour, Dem Appelz, or Rhubarb Sour on pages 57, 67, and 70, respectively)
¼ cup (2 fl oz/60 ml) champagne vinegar
1 tablespoon smooth Dijon mustard
2½ cups (21 fl oz/600 ml) canola oil
2 tablespoons Old Bay Seasoning (see glossary)
1 tablespoon white miso paste
juice of 1 lemon

In a blender or food processor, combine the egg yolks, vinegar, mustard, and 2 tablespoons of water until smooth.

With the motor running, slowly pour in the canola oil until the mixture thickens. If it's too thick, add another 2 tablespoons of water—the mixture should be homogeneous, with a thick, creamy texture.

Transfer to a bowl and mix in the Old Bay Seasoning and miso paste. Dip your finger in to taste, then season with the lemon juice and some sea salt if necessary. A crack of black pepper wouldn't go astray.

The mayo will keep in an airtight container in the fridge for up to 1 week.

DRY RANCH SPICE

This is awesome on baked potatoes, steamed potatoes, roasted potatoes, radishes, steak...you get the idea. [Makes about 1¼ cups/7 oz/200 g]

¼ cup (1¾ oz/50 g) onion flakes
1 tablespoon chili flakes
¼ cup (1¾ oz/50 g) dried dill
¼ cup (1¾ oz/50 g) garlic granules
1 tablespoon finely ground black pepper
2 tablespoons citric acid
2 teaspoons fine sea salt
1 teaspoon ground espelette pepper (see glossary)

Grind the onion flakes, chili flakes, and dill in a coffee grinder (don't make coffee afterward). Alternatively, you could use a mortar and pestle for this. Transfer the spices to a mixing bowl.

Add the remaining ingredients and mix well to combine.

Store in an airtight container until required; the spice mix will keep indefinitely in a cool dark place.

MUSTARD BARBECUE SAUCE

Most North Carolina barbecue sauce is mustard-based—the perfect accompaniment to fattier cuts of meat like pulled pork and lamb ribs. Match the fat to the meat, so if serving the sauce with lamb ribs, use lamb fat; if serving with pulled pork, use pork fat. [Makes 4 cups/32 fl oz/1 liter]

Melt the fat in a large, heavy-based saucepan. Add the onion and garlic; allow to sweat and cook over medium heat for about 15 minutes, until the onion becomes translucent and the edges are slightly brown.

Stir in the vinegar and Worcestershire sauce, and cook for about 5 minutes, until reduced by half. Add the spices and cook for another 5 minutes.

Stir in the remaining ingredients and cook the mixture over low heat for 30 minutes. Season to taste with sea salt and freshly ground black pepper.

The sauce will keep in an airtight container in the fridge for up to 2 weeks.

½ cup (4½ oz/125 g) animal fat (see Rendering Fat, pages 244–245)
1 brown onion, finely chopped
6 garlic cloves, finely chopped
½ cup (4 fl oz/125 ml) apple cider vinegar
125 ml (4 fl oz/½ cup) Worcestershire sauce
1 tablespoon mustard powder
2 tablespoons smoked paprika
1 teaspoon cayenne pepper
1 teaspoon chili flakes, crushed
2 tablespoons light brown sugar
1 cup (8 oz/250 g) ketchup
1 cup (8 oz/250 g) Dijon mustard

TOGARASHI SALT

Togarashi ticks all the boxes. A little bit sweet, a little bit salty, slightly seedy, and somewhat nutty. It makes you want to lick your fingers. Win! Use it to season ham, corn, popcorn, clams (vongole).
[Makes about 1½ cups/12 oz/350 g]

Combine all the ingredients, mixing well. Store in an airtight container in a cool, dry place. Your togarashi salt will keep pretty much forever.

1 cup (3½ oz/100 g) shichimi togarashi (see glossary)
1 cup (8 oz/250 g) sea salt
1 tablespoon superfine sugar

S'MORES
SWEET POTATO PIES WITH MARSHMALLOW TOPS
APPLE CRISP WITH FROZEN CUSTARD
DOUGHNUT ICE CREAM-STUFFED DOUGHNUTS
BUNGALOW ICE CREAM
NAOMI'S GRANDMA'S LEMON TART
STONE FRUIT BUCKLE
GERI'S GINGER CAKE
FRANNY'S STICKY BUNS
Q'S CHIC-CHOP ICE CREAM SANDWICHES
BANANA CREAM PIE
CHEESECAKE SUNDAE
MILKSHAKES

S'MORES

Every summer, my cousins and I would toast marshmallows around the fire. Marshmallows get to a point where they're perfectly golden on the outside but liquid on the inside, so they'll slide right off your toasting stick and onto your graham cracker.

I used to rest my graham cracker and chocolate on a log close to the fire, so that by the time my mallow was ready, the heat had softened the chocolate and made it a perfect match for the molten marshmallow.

Of course, if it suits you better, it's permissible to skip making the crackers entirely and purchase some from your local store. [Makes 8]

GRAHAM CRACKERS

1 cup (8 oz/250 g) butter, softened
¾ cup (5¾ oz/165 g) firmly packed
   light brown sugar
¼ cup (3¼ oz/90 g) honey
1 teaspoon sea salt
1 cup (5½ oz/150 g) all-purpose flour
1 cup (3½ oz/100 g) almond meal
¾ cup (2¼ oz/60 g) wheat germ
1 teaspoon baking soda
1 teaspoon ground cinnamon

In a mixing bowl, beat the butter, sugar, honey, and sea salt until pale and creamy using electric beaters; this will take about 4 minutes. Add the remaining ingredients and mix until thoroughly combined.

Turn out onto a floured work surface. Divide the dough into four equal portions. Roll out each portion between sheets of parchment paper into a 4 x 8 inch (10 x 20 cm) rectangle. Layer the portions on top of each other with parchment sheets in between, and refrigerate for about 30 minutes, or until chilled.

Preheat the oven to 300°F (150°C). Discard the top layer of parchment paper and separate the dough portions, leaving each on a sheet of parchment paper. Trim the dough edges, then score each portion into four smaller rectangles, each measuring about 2 x 4 inches (5 x 10 cm). Dock each rectangle with a fork five times.

Transfer each portion (still on its sheet of parchment paper) to a baking tray. Bake for 8–10 minutes, or until golden brown. Cool on a wire rack, then break each piece along the score marks into four smaller rectangles.

You want these crackers to stay crisp, so for best results bake them close to serving time; at most, they will keep only a day or two in an airtight container in a cool, dark place.

MARSHMALLOWS

½ cup (2¼ oz/60 g) confectioners' sugar, sifted

½ cup (2¼ oz/60 g) cornstarch

1 tablespoon glucose (available online, if not in your local specialty store)

2 cups (1 lb/450 g) superfine sugar

3 egg whites

1½ teaspoons (⅙ oz/7 g) powdered gelatin

EQUIPMENT
sugar thermometer

Spray a baking dish with cooking oil, then dust with 1 tablespoon of the confectioners' sugar. Put the remaining confectioners' sugar in a large bowl, mix the cornstarch through, and set aside for dusting the marshmallows.

Combine the glucose, superfine sugar, and a generous ¾ cup (7 fl oz/200 ml) of water in a saucepan, and heat until the sugar has dissolved. Continue cooking until the mixture reaches 250°F (120°C) on a sugar thermometer.

Meanwhile, using an electric mixer fitted with a whisk attachment, beat the egg whites until stiff peaks form. Now gradually add the hot glucose syrup; when all the sugar is incorporated, the egg whites will be shiny, tacky, and fluffy. Continue whipping for 10 minutes on high speed until the mixture is cool.

Meanwhile, dissolve the gelatin in a generous ¾ cup (7 fl oz/200 ml) of water and let it "bloom" for 7–8 minutes. Microwave at 20-second intervals until the gelatin is completely dissolved and warm; do not allow it to boil. Working quickly, pour the gelatin mixture into the egg whites while they're still being whipped.

Pour the egg white mixture into the prepared baking dish. Press down to level out, then dust with 1 tablespoon of the cornstarch mixture. Leave at room temperature for a few hours, or until completely cool and solidified.

Turn the marshmallow out onto a cutting board. Cut into eight squares the same size as the graham crackers, then toss into the remaining cornstarch mixture.

The marshmallows can be made up to a day ahead and stored in an airtight container in a cool, dark place.

TO SERVE
Chocolate bars

TO ASSEMBLE
Take your favorite chocolate bar, and snap it into squares the same size as your graham crackers.

Turn the oven broiler up high. Grab a baking tray and keep it handy.

Top half of the graham crackers with a marshmallow, and the remaining half with the chocolate.

Place them on the baking tray and broil until the marshmallow is torched and the chocolate is half melted. Sandwich the two halves together and get ready to indulge!

SWEET POTATO PIES with MARSHMALLOW TOPS

My favorite dessert that must be featured in my favorite holiday, Thanksgiving. The Aussies don't know what they're missing out on. [Serves 6]

To make the dough, process the flour, salt, and sugar in a food processor until pea-sized crumbs form. Add the butter in batches, pulsing to a granular consistency. Turn out into a bowl. Add the chilled water in batches, mixing by hand until the dough is just combined. Wrap in plastic wrap and refrigerate for 1 hour.

Roll out the dough on a floured surface to about ⅛ inch (3 mm) thick. Press into a 9½-inch (24 cm) floured pie dish, or into six 4-inch (10 cm) floured dishes. Trim off the excess, then crimp the edge and prick the base with a fork. Freeze for 15–20 minutes, to solidify the butter in the pastry.

Meanwhile, start preparing the filling. Preheat the oven to 350°F (180°C). Put the sweet potatoes on a baking tray and bake for 45 minutes to 1 hour, or until tender. Remove from the oven and leave to cool.

Turn the oven down to 315°F (160°C). Cover the dough with a sheet of parchment paper, then weigh the paper down with baking beads, dried beans, or uncooked rice. Blind bake* a large pie for 25–30 minutes, or the smaller ones for about 15 minutes, or until the pastry is golden.

Meanwhile, finish off the filling. Cut the sweet potatoes in half and scoop the flesh into a food processor. Add the spices, salt, sugar, and vanilla seeds, and purée until smooth. Add the eggs one at a time, then the condensed milk—the batter should be thick, not runny.

Turn the oven down to 300°F (150°C). Pour the filling into the pre-baked pie crust and bake for 45 minutes, or until set into a custard. Drizzle with the golden syrup and bake for a final 15 minutes. Remove from the oven and leave to cool for 30 minutes.

Top the pie with the whipped marshmallow, using a spatula to create meringue-like peaks. Now refrigerate the pie for at least 4 hours, to set the marshmallow and filling.

Torch the marshmallow topping with a kitchen blowtorch until golden brown, as you would a meringue. Enjoy the same day, drizzled with extra golden syrup.

* Blind baking is the process of baking a pie crust before the filling is added.

DOUGH
- 1½ cups (8 oz/225 g) all-purpose flour
- ½ teaspoon sea salt
- 2 tablespoons superfine sugar
- 11 tablespoons (5½ oz/160 g) cold butter, diced
- ½ cup (4 fl oz/125 ml) chilled water

FILLING
- 3 large sweet potatoes, skins on
- 2 tablespoons ground cinnamon
- 2 teaspoons ground ginger
- 1 teaspoon ground mace
- 1 teaspoon freshly grated nutmeg
- ½ teaspoon ground allspice
- 2 teaspoons sea salt
- 1 cup (8 oz/230 g) firmly packed light brown sugar
- 1 vanilla bean, split in half lengthwise, seeds scraped
- 4 eggs
- 1 cup (8 oz/250 g) sweetened condensed milk

TOPPING
- ¼ cup (3¼ oz/90 g) golden syrup or molasses, plus extra to serve
- 1 batch of whipped marshmallow (prepared following the recipe on page 209, up until the gelatin is added)

EQUIPMENT
sugar thermometer
kitchen blowtorch

APPLE CRISP with FROZEN CUSTARD

Every birthday as kids we got to pick our dessert, and I would always ask for this. Mom would make it with more topping than apple, and the smell would fill the entire house. She'd never serve it with frozen custard, though; I doubt she'll approve of this combo! You'll have some frozen custard left over, most likely. No problem, as it will keep in the freezer for a few weeks and is great with waffles and doughnuts. [Serves 6]

FROZEN CUSTARD
5 egg yolks
½ cup (4 oz/115 g) superfine
    sugar
2 cups (17 fl oz/500 ml) whipping
    cream (35% fat)

APPLE FILLING
12 Granny Smith apples, peeled,
    cored, and cut into eighths
1 cup (8 oz/230 g) firmly packed
    light brown sugar
½ cup (2¼ oz/60 g) cornstarch
2 teaspoons ground cinnamon
½ teaspoon freshly grated nutmeg
1 vanilla bean, split in half
    lengthwise, seeds scraped
zest and juice of 1 lemon
scant ½ cup (3½ fl oz/100 ml)
    apple cider
¼ cup (1½ fl oz/50 ml) maple
    syrup

OAT TOPPING
2 cups (7 oz/200 g) rolled oats
1½ cups (11½ oz/330 g) firmly
    packed light brown sugar
1 cup (5½ oz/150 g) all-purpose
    flour
14 tablespoons (7 oz/200 g)
    butter, chilled and diced

Start by making the frozen custard. In a heatproof bowl, mix the egg yolks and half the sugar until combined.

In a saucepan, bring the remaining sugar and half the cream to a boil.

Slowly pour the hot cream over the egg yolk mixture, to temper the yolks. Pour the egg yolk mixture into the saucepan, then cook the mixture over low heat, stirring constantly until the mixture is thick enough to coat the back of a spoon. Cover and refrigerate for about 2 hours, until it sets into a custard.

Using an electric mixer, whip the remaining cream until soft peaks form, then fold the cream through the chilled custard. Transfer to a freezer-proof container and freeze for at least 1 hour, or until required; the custard can be frozen for several weeks.

When you're ready to cook your dessert, preheat the oven to 325°F (170°C). In a bowl, toss all the apple filling ingredients until the apples are coated. Transfer to a large baking dish, or six 4½-inch (12 cm) dishes or ramekins.

In another bowl, combine the topping ingredients, rubbing them together with your fingertips until all the butter is incorporated—the consistency should be crumbly, with pea-sized crumbs, but on the moist side.

Evenly disperse the oat topping over the apples, then bake for 1 hour. The apples will break down, the liquid will melt into the topping, and it will be really crispy on top.

Remove from the oven and set aside until cool enough to handle easily. Spoon the frozen custard on top and devour.

DOUGHNUT ICE CREAM-STUFFED DOUGHNUTS

I had a small obsession with Dunkin' Donuts when I first started out as a chef, usually at about midnight when I was driving home—a medium coffee, light and sweet, and two glazed doughnuts. These made a perfect midnight snack. Creamy, frozen doughnuts. Mmmmm. You'll really need an ice cream machine for this one. [Serves 6]

vegetable oil, for deep-frying

DOUGHNUT ICE CREAM
1 cup (8 fl oz/250 ml) milk
1 cup (8 fl oz/250 ml) whipping
    cream (35% fat)
½ cup (4 oz/115 g) superfine
    sugar
1 vanilla bean, split in half
    lengthwise, seeds scraped
½ teaspoon ground cinnamon
6 ready-made glazed doughnuts
7 eggs

DOUGHNUT BALLS
2 lb 4 oz (1 kg) ricotta cheese
1 cup (8 oz/230 g) superfine sugar,
    plus extra for dusting
2 vanilla beans, split in half
    lengthwise, seeds scraped
3 cups (1 lb/450 g) all-purpose
    flour
5 eggs
2 teaspoons baking powder

EQUIPMENT
ice cream machine
sugar thermometer
ice-cream scoop with a lever

To make the ice cream, bring the milk, cream, sugar, vanilla seeds, and cinnamon to a boil in a large saucepan. Add the whole doughnuts and immediately remove from the heat. Cover with a lid and cool to room temperature.

Pour the mixture through a fine mesh sieve into a saucepan, extracting as much liquid as possible by using the back of a ladle to push the liquid through. Any doughnut particles that make it through the sieve are welcome to stay, but discard the solids in the sieve. Bring the mixture to a boil, then remove from the heat.

Using an electric mixer fitted with a whisk attachment, whip the eggs for about 10 minutes, until pale, creamy, and tripled in volume. Slowly stream in the simmered doughnut milk, whisking on low until the custard thickens.

Transfer the custard to the freezer, chilling as quickly as possible. Churn in your ice cream machine according to the manufacturer's instructions.

To make the doughnut balls, put the ricotta, sugar, vanilla seeds, flour, eggs, and baking powder in a mixing bowl. Using an electric mixer fitted with a paddle attachment, beat until the mixture is smooth, with no lumps. Cover and refrigerate for at least 1 hour.

In a deep fryer or heavy-based saucepan, heat at least 2 inches (5 cm) of vegetable oil to 285°F (140°C). Dip an ice cream scoop into the hot oil, then into the doughnut batter. With a level top, release the batter balls into the oil. Fry for 3 minutes on each side (they'll turn over by themselves). Toss the hot doughnuts in lots of extra sugar, then cool on a baking tray.

To serve, cut the doughnut balls in half and stuff with the doughnut ice cream. It doesn't have to be pretty! There are two reasons to do this: to get fat and to get happy.

BUNGALOW ICE CREAM

My Uncle Jeff made this one summer, but he swears he never did. (I blame his memory lapse on the beer keg on tap.) I vividly remember he spun it on a stainless steel table to the left of the bungalow. When the ice cream was done, it was a beautiful rose color, and the strawberries were frozen and hard. I also remember there wasn't enough for all the cousins! [Serves 6]

Start by making the strawberry syrup. Half-fill a saucepan with water, and heat until simmering.

Meanwhile, combine the strawberries, sugar, salt, and vanilla seeds in a heatproof bowl that will fit snugly over the saucepan. Massage the ingredients into the strawberries.

Cover the bowl tightly with aluminum foil, then place over the simmering water, making sure the base of the bowl is sitting a good 3 inches (7.5 cm) above the water. Simmer for 1 hour; the mixture should become a clear pink color, and of a syrupy consistency.

Strain the strawberry syrup through a fine mesh sieve, reserving the strawberries; you should end up with about 2 cups (17 fl oz/500 ml) of syrup. Refrigerate the syrup and strawberries separately for a few hours, until really cold.

To make the ice cream, combine the chilled strawberry syrup, crème fraîche, vanilla seeds, sugar, and egg yolks in a heatproof bowl and mix until homogeneous.

In a large saucepan, heat the cream and milk until almost boiling (not just simmering). Slowly add half the milk mixture to the syrup mixture, a ladle at a time, until it has been incorporated. Now add all the syrup mixture to the milk mixture remaining in the pan.

Cook over low heat, stirring constantly with a rubber spatula, doing your best not to incorporate air by whisking. Cook for 10–12 minutes, or until the mixture coats the back of a spoon, which means the egg yolks have set. Refrigerate for several hours, until really cold.

In a food processor, blend the reserved strawberries with the fresh strawberries and pulse until chunky. Add to the chilled ice cream mixture.

Churn in your ice cream machine according to the manufacturer's instructions. Enjoy as fresh as possible.

9 oz (250 g) strawberries, green hulls removed

STRAWBERRY SYRUP

1 lb 2 oz (500 g) strawberries, green hulls removed
1 cup (8 oz/230 g) superfine sugar
1 teaspoon sea salt
1 vanilla bean, split in half lengthwise, seeds scraped

ICE CREAM

1 cup (8 oz/250 g) crème fraîche (see glossary) or sour cream
1 vanilla bean, split in half lengthwise, seeds scraped
1 cup (8 oz/230 g) superfine sugar
8 egg yolks
3 cups (24 fl oz/750 ml) whipping cream (35% fat)
2 cups (17 fl oz/500 ml) whole milk

EQUIPMENT
ice cream machine

MY GRANDMA AIN'T NO TART

My grandma lived in Canowindra, a little country town in the Western Tablelands of New South Wales, Australia. These days it's a cozy collective of wineries, antique stores, and art galleries, but back when we were kids, the most exciting thing that ever happened was the mouse plague that hit one year.

Worse still, our grandfather had been Canowindra's Anglican minister, so while it might have been the Easter school holidays when we visited, there was no chance we were getting a break from church as well. Eyes glazed, we would endure the Easter services knowing that our small reward would be Grandma's lemon meringue tart, which was cooling on the windowsill for dessert.

Except it wasn't really a tart. It was lemon meringue minus the tart. A tartless meringue, if you will. Nobody knows why my grandma didn't make the tart part. She wasn't a woman to cut corners; she darned socks, for heaven's sake. But that's the way she made it, and as life so often teaches us, I didn't think to ask her until it was too late.

Luckily for you, however, Gregory knows all about tarts, so we've paired my grandmother's lemon filling with my husband's tart. So to speak.

Grandma's ginger cake also made the cut for this book, and it's the only cake ever considered for a Hart family celebration. This could be because it tastes really good, but it's more likely to be because it's pretty hard to screw up, even if you don't own a mixer. Trust me.

Don't be fooled by the inclusion of the choc-chip (or rather, chic-chop) ice cream sandwiches. Yes, more often than not they're a dessert for those who can measure their age in single digits, but they're actually the perfect sweet treat for a cocktail party—one hand for your drink, one hand for your dessert. No spoon required. We tested the theory at our wedding and it worked brilliantly. Not an ice cream–stained party dress in sight.

NAOMI'S GRANDMA'S LEMON TART

You could muck around with the citrus here and use limes or yuzu instead of lemon. You may need to adjust the sugar content, so remember to sample the lemon curd before pouring it into the tart. Adorn the tart however you fancy: some thin lemon slices maybe, or perhaps a sprinkling of marigold petals. The tart is enhanced, of course, with whipped cream. [Serves 6]

Preheat the oven to 325°F (170°C).

To make the tart base, put the oats, flour, and sugar in a bowl. Add the diced butter and mix together using your fingertips, until the consistency is granular and you have pea-sized crumbs. Spread the mixture out on a baking tray and bake for 10 minutes. Remove from the oven and leave to cool.

Put the baked oat crumbs in a food processor and pulse to a uniform consistency. Transfer to a bowl, add the melted butter, and mix to combine. Press into a tart (flan) pan with a removable base, then refrigerate.

To make the lemon curd, set up a double boiler, or set a heatproof bowl over a saucepan of simmering water, ensuring the base of the bowl isn't touching the water.

In the top boiler or heatproof bowl, combine the lemon zest, lemon juice, sugar, and egg yolks. Bring to a simmer, then cook, whisking frequently, for 10–12 minutes, or until the mixture is thick and custardlike, and coats the back of a spoon. Remove from the heat, then slowly emulsify the cold butter into the lemon curd until incorporated.

Pour the mixture neatly into the tart shell, avoiding the rim. Refrigerate for about 4 hours, or until set.

Enjoy the tart the same day; any leftovers will keep in an airtight container in the fridge for 2 days.

TART BASE

2 cups (7 oz/200 g) rolled oats

1 cup (5½ oz/150 g) all-purpose flour

1 cup (8 oz/230 g) firmly packed light or dark brown sugar

14 tablespoons (7 oz/200 g) butter, chilled and diced, plus an extra 7 tablespoons (3½ oz/100 g) butter, melted

LEMON CURD

zest and juice of 12 lemons; you'll need about 1 cup (8 fl oz/250 ml) juice

1 cup (8 oz/230 g) superfine sugar

12 egg yolks

1 cup (8 oz/250 g) butter, chilled and diced

STONE FRUIT BUCKLE

The definitions go like this: a tart has a cookie crust; a crumble has an oat top; a cobbler is covered with an egg, flour, and sugar mix; and a buckle is a batter layered with fruit. [Serves 6]

10 apricots, quartered and pitted

1 lb 2 oz (500 g) cherries, halved and pitted

4 nectarines, quartered and pitted

4 peaches, quartered and pitted

6 plums, quartered and pitted

2 vanilla beans, split in half lengthwise, seeds scraped

1 cup (8 oz/230 g) superfine sugar

5 lemon thyme sprigs, leaves picked

1 cup (4½ oz/125 g) cornstarch

2 teaspoons sea salt

1 cup (4½ oz/125 g) confectioners' sugar

3 sticks (12 oz/350 g) butter at room temperature, chopped

4 eggs at room temperature

2 cups (7 oz/200 g) almond meal

2 teaspoons baking powder

1 cup (8 oz/ 230 g) firmly packed light or dark brown sugar

1 cup (5½ oz/150 g) all-purpose flour

Preheat the oven to 315°F (160°C). Grease and flour a baking dish.

Place all the fruit in a bowl. In a separate bowl, combine the vanilla seeds, superfine sugar, lemon thyme, cornstarch, and salt. Rub the sugar mixture together, then pour over the fruit and toss to combine. Set aside.

Put the confectioners' sugar and 14 tablespoons (7 oz/ 200 g) of the butter in a bowl. Using electric beaters, mix until pale in color. Add the eggs one at a time, beating until thoroughly incorporated, then fold in the almond meal and baking powder.

Layer half the fruit mixture in the prepared baking dish, then spoon half the batter on top. Repeat.

In a bowl, using your fingertips, mix the remaining butter with the brown sugar and flour until the consistency is granular and you have pea-sized crumbs. Spread the mixture over the buckle and bake for 1 hour.

Leave to rest in the oven for 15 minutes before serving. The fruit buckle is wonderful eaten warm, but will keep in the fridge for a few days.

GERI'S GINGER CAKE

Naomi used to call her grandma Geri, short for "geriatric." It was a term of endearment, I'm assured. Geri passed away before I could meet her, just after Naomi and I started dating, but Naomi tells me this cake is just like her—spicy, warm, and reliable. [Serves 6]

Preheat the oven to 350°F (180°C). Grease and line a 9-inch (23 cm) square cake pan.

In a bowl, cream the margarine, golden syrup, and sugar using electric beaters. Add two of the eggs, mixing to combine.

Sift 1 cup (5½ oz/150 g) of the flour with the spices, then add to the batter and mix until combined. Add the remaining eggs and mix to combine. Now sift in another 1 cup (5½ oz/150 g) of the flour and mix to combine.

Combine the baking soda and milk, mixing well. Working in batches, add the milk mixture to the batter, alternating with the remaining flour, mixing to combine.

Pour the batter into the prepared cake pan. Bake on the middle rack of the oven for about 1 hour, or until a skewer inserted in the center of the cake comes out clean.

The cake is fabulous warm, but will keep for up to 3 days in an airtight container in the pantry.

1 cup (8 oz/250 g) margarine
1 cup (12 oz/350 g) golden syrup
  or molasses
1 cup (8 oz/230 g) superfine sugar
4 eggs
3 cups (1 lb/450 g) all-purpose
  flour
3 teaspoons ground ginger
3 teaspoons ground cinnamon
2 teaspoons freshly grated
  nutmeg
1 teaspoon baking soda
1 cup (8 fl oz/250 ml) milk, soured
  with a splash of vinegar

FRANNY'S STICKY BUNS

My mom has been making these sticky buns every Christmas since 1983. She tinkered with the original recipe, increasing the topping until we were all happy with the quantity. She doesn't even bother taking them out of the baking pan—that's how fast they're gone. Definitely something I miss, being away from home. [Makes 12]

2¼ teaspoons dried yeast
¼ cup (2 fl oz/60 ml) warm water
⅔ cup (5½ fl oz/170 ml) milk,
    boiled then cooled
¼ cup (2¼ oz/60 g) butter, melted
¼ cup (2 oz/55 g) sugar
1 teaspoon sea salt
4 egg yolks
3¼ cups (1 lb 1 oz/485 g)
    all-purpose flour
cold butter, for slathering over
    the hot buns

TOPPING
7 tablespoons (3½ oz/100 g)
    butter, softened
1 cup (4 oz/115 g) chopped
    pecans
1 tablespoon ground cinnamon
1½ cups (12 oz/345 g) firmly
    packed light or dark brown
    sugar
¼ cup (3¼ oz/90 g) honey
1 tablespoon natural vanilla
    extract

In a clean, dry bowl, combine the yeast and warm water. Let stand for 10–15 minutes, until frothy.

In the bowl of an electric mixer fitted with a dough hook, combine the milk, butter, sugar, and salt. Add the yeast mixture. Carefully add the egg yolks, then the flour, combining thoroughly.

Turn the dough out onto a floured surface and knead for 2 minutes. Roll out the dough to a square ¾ inch (2 cm) thick. For the topping, spoon half the butter evenly over the dough, then sprinkle with the pecans, cinnamon, and 1 cup (8 oz/230 g) of the sugar. Roll up the dough tightly, then slice into 12 scrolls.

Spoon the remaining butter, sugar, honey, and vanilla onto a baking tray. Heat the baking tray over low heat until the butter has melted, stirring the mixture to distribute it evenly over the tray. Lay the scrolls flat in the glazed baking tray, in four rows of three. Cover with parchment paper or plastic wrap. Refrigerate for at least 12 hours (this is called "retarding," which is the opposite of proofing; it develops flavor by allowing the yeast to penetrate the dough.)

Remove the scrolls from the fridge and leave to proof in a warm place in the kitchen for 1½ hours, or until doubled in size (the buns will be touching each other).

Preheat the oven to 310°F (155°C). Transfer the buns to the oven and bake for 40 minutes.

Meanwhile, cover your favorite chopping board with foil, crimping up the sides to form a boundary (to catch the hot caramel from the buns). Remove the baking tray from the oven, then immediately, while the scrolls are still hot, turn them out onto the foil-covered chopping board; the caramel will cascade down the sides of the scrolls.

Eat the scrolls screaming hot; the only thing that saves you burning the roof of your mouth is slapping cold butter on top. Any scrolls that don't disappear at once will keep for 1–2 days in an airtight container in the pantry.

Q'S CHIC-CHOP ICE CREAM SANDWICHES

Q and Naomi make cookies ("chic-chop cookies," as Q used to call them when she was a tiny thing) on a semi-regular basis. They, however, do not use a recipe. To increase your chances of success, I recommend you do. All measurements are vague and portioned with the hands of a toddler.

[Makes 6 large cookies]

Preheat the oven to 350°F (180°C). Grease and line two baking trays.

To make the cookies, put all the ingredients in a bowl and mix together. We don't own a mixing machine, so Naomi and Q just use a wooden spoon.

Add more of whatever, if you think it's necessary. Test by making a ball and seeing if it stays together.

Form the cookies into any shape you like and watch them bake for 10 minutes or so while you sit on the floor in front of the oven.

Let them cool, then just before serving, pack as much ice cream between the cookies as you can—layering with different flavors if you've got them.

Serve with a glass of milk and a straw.

These cookies shouldn't last more than a day, only because you've eaten them all…

CHIC-CHOP COOKIES
½ **cup (4 fl oz/125 ml) coconut oil**
½ **cup (4 oz/115 g) superfine sugar**
1¾ **cups (9¼ oz/260 g) self-rising whole-wheat flour**
1 egg
natural vanilla extract (measured with the delicate pour of a three-year-old)
knob of butter, for binding
most of a 9 oz (250 g) bag of chocolate chips (depending on how many get eaten during mixing)

TO SERVE
your favorite ice cream

BANANA CREAM PIE

This baby (pictured on pages 232–233) is from our pastry chef Andrew Bowden (or Andy Bowdy, as he's better known), who has been with us since day one. The pies at Hartsyard started out confined to a jar, and are now monstrosities on a plate. The flavors change often, yet all hold to Andy's theory that everything tastes better with *a lot* of fresh cream. [Serves 6]

CHOCOLATE CRUMBS

14 tablespoons (7 oz/200 g) butter
1¾ cups (9¼ oz/260 g) all-purpose flour
1⅓ cups (9 oz/250 g) superfine sugar
1⅓ cups (5¼ oz/145 g) unsweetened cocoa powder
1 tablespoon cornstarch
2 teaspoons sea salt

Preheat the oven to 325°F (170°C). Line a baking tray with parchment paper.

Melt the butter in a small saucepan.

Place all the remaining ingredients in a mixing bowl. Mix the melted butter through, until the mixture forms crumbs.

Spread the crumbs over the baking tray and bake for 25 minutes. Remove from the oven and leave to cool; the crumbs will crisp up as they cool.

The crumbs can be stored in an airtight container in the pantry for up to 2 weeks.

CHOCOLATE SAUCE

1 cup (8 fl oz/250 ml) whipping cream (35% fat)
1 cup (12 oz/375 g) glucose (available online, if not in your local specialty store)
½ cup (3¼ oz/95 g) superfine sugar
generous ½ cup (2½ oz/70 g) unsweetened cocoa powder
¾ cup (3¾ oz/110 g) chopped dark chocolate
¾ teaspoon sea salt

Place the cream, glucose, and sugar in a saucepan. Bring to a boil, then reduce the heat to a simmer.

Add the cocoa powder, chocolate, and salt and stir thoroughly. Cook for an additional 5 minutes, stirring constantly, until the sauce becomes smooth and glossy.

Remove from the heat and leave to cool. Depending on the expiration date of the cream, the sauce can be made a few days ahead and refrigerated in an airtight container until needed.

BANANA CAKE

8 tablespoons (3¾ oz/110 g) butter, chopped
½ cup (4 oz/115 g) superfine sugar
2 eggs
14 oz (400 g) bananas, chopped
⅓ cup (2½ fl oz/80 ml) buttermilk
1½ cups (8 oz/225 g) self-rising flour
pinch of sea salt

Preheat the oven to 375°F (190°C).

In a bowl, beat the butter and sugar together using electric beaters, until pale and creamy. Beat in the eggs one at a time, until completely incorporated. Beat in the bananas, followed by the buttermilk. Now fold the flour and the salt through until just combined.

Pour the batter into a greased cake pan (any style and size will do, as we'll be breaking up the cake later on).

Bake for about 25 minutes, or until the cake is golden and a skewer inserted in the center comes out clean.

This cake can be made a day or two ahead, and kept in an airtight container until required.

BANANA CUSTARD

ice cubes
5 egg yolks
3 cups (24 fl oz/720 ml) milk
⅔ cup (5 oz/140 g) sugar
⅓ cup (1½ oz/40 g) cornstarch
½ teaspoon sea salt
1 lb (450 g) bananas, chopped

Prepare an ice bath by pouring cold water into a heatproof bowl and adding lots of ice cubes.

Place all the remaining ingredients in a bender and blitz until smooth.

Transfer the mixture to a saucepan and cook over medium heat for about 10 minutes, or until the mixture thickens. Cool immediately by plunging the saucepan into the ice bath.

The custard will set when it cools, so it's best made not too long before serving the pie.

WHIPPED CREAM

4 cups (32 fl oz/1 liter) whipping cream (35% fat)
½ cup (3½ oz/100 g) sugar
1 vanilla bean, split in half lengthwise, seeds scraped

Immediately before serving, place the cream, sugar, and vanilla seeds in a large bowl. Using electric beaters, whip to stiff peaks.

TO SERVE

2 tablespoons (1 oz/30 g) butter, melted
2 bananas, roughly chopped
grated dark chocolate, to garnish

TO ASSEMBLE

Take your chocolate crumbs and mix the melted butter through. Press the crumbs into a 10-inch (25 cm) pie pan to make a pie crust.

Pour the cooled banana custard into the pie crust. Scatter over the chopped bananas. Tear the banana cake into 1-inch (2.5 cm) chunks and push them into the custard. Cover with the whipped cream.

Drizzle the chocolate sauce all over the top and finish with some grated dark chocolate.

The pie is best enjoyed straight away, as the whipped cream won't hold for long.

CHEESECAKE SUNDAE

Another Andy special, this is really a combo of two of the original desserts on our menu: the deep-fried cheesecake, and the peanut butter and banana sundae. The first dessert Andy misses; the second one we can't get rid of on account of its popularity. If you don't have an ice cream machine, you don't have to miss out. Just buy your favorite vanilla ice cream instead of making the Cheesecake Ice Cream on page 236. [Serves 6]

SALTED CARAMEL

2 cups (14 oz/400 g) superfine sugar
7 tablespoons (5½ oz/150 g) glucose
11 tablespoons (5½ oz/150 g) butter, chopped
2 cups (17 fl oz/500 ml) whipping cream (35% fat)
1 tablespoon sea salt

Place the sugar and glucose in a saucepan with 1 tablespoon water. Place on the stove over high heat and cook until the mixture turns a dark caramel color; this can happen quite quickly, or can take as long as it wants to.

Working quickly, and with the pan still on the stove, add the chopped butter, stirring vigorously, ensuring everything is fully incorporated into a homogeneous mixture.

Stir the cream through. Add the salt and leave to cool. As good as it may smell, it's best not to stick your finger in until the caramel has cooled completely—sugar burns tend to wreck your day!

The caramel can be made up to 1 week ahead; store it in an airtight container in the fridge until required.

PASSION FRUIT CURD

½ cup (3½ fl oz/100 ml) passion fruit juice
2 eggs
½ cup (3½ oz/100 g) superfine sugar
11 tablespoons (5½ oz/150 g) butter at room temperature, chopped

Place the passion fruit juice, eggs, and sugar in a heatproof bowl. Set the bowl over a saucepan of simmering water, ensuring the base of the bowl isn't touching the water.

Stirring constantly with a whisk, cook until the mixture is thick and fluffy; this can take up to 10 minutes.

While the pan is still on the stove, stir the butter through, then remove from the heat and leave to cool.

The passion fruit curd can be made up to 1 week ahead; keep in an airtight container in the fridge until required.

CHEESECAKE

1 lb 5 oz (600 g) cream cheese
2 cups (14 oz/400 g) sugar
4 eggs
1 vanilla bean, split in half lengthwise, seeds scraped
1½ tablespoons cornstarch
generous ¼ cup (2¼ fl oz/70 ml) milk
grated zest of 1 lemon

Preheat the oven to 325°F (170°C). Find a baking tray that is at least 3¼ inches (8 cm) deep and line it with parchment paper.

In a mixing bowl, beat the cream cheese and sugar together until smooth, using electric beaters. Beat in the eggs one at a time, until completely incorporated.

CONTINUED ON THE NEXT PAGE... ▶▶▶▶

Add the vanilla seeds, cornstarch, milk, and lemon zest, and beat until smooth.

Transfer to the lined tray and bake for about 30 minutes, or until the mixture has set.

Remove from the oven and leave to cool, then chill in the fridge until completely cold. The cheesecake can be made up to 3 days ahead; refrigerate in an airtight container until needed.

CHEESECAKE ICE CREAM

1 cup (8 fl oz/250 ml) milk
¼ cup (1½ fl oz/50 ml) whipping cream (35% fat)
¾ cup (7 oz/200 g) Cheesecake (see page 235; reserve the rest for assembling the dessert)
¼ cup (1 oz/30 g) milk powder
½ teaspoon sea salt

EQUIPMENT
ice cream machine

Place all the ingredients in a blender and blitz until smooth. Transfer to an ice cream machine and churn according to the manufacturer's instructions. The ice cream can be made a day or two ahead and kept frozen until required.

CARAMEL POPCORN

⅔ cup (5 oz/145 g) superfine sugar
4 cups popcorn
sea salt, to taste

Place the sugar in a saucepan large enough to hold all the popcorn. Cook over high heat until the mixture turns a light caramel color. Remove from the heat, pour in the popcorn, and fold through until completely coated.

Pour the popcorn onto a sheet of parchment paper, season with sea salt, and allow to cool.

The popcorn can be made up to 2 days ahead. Store in an airtight container in the pantry until needed.

BATTER
1½ cups (8 oz/225 g) self-rising flour
¼ cup (2 oz/55 g) superfine sugar
1 cup (8 fl oz/250 ml) buttermilk
1 egg
1¾ oz (50 g) frozen blueberries

Place all the ingredients in a mixing bowl and beat until smooth, using electric beaters, or whisking by hand. Cover and chill in the fridge for 1 hour before using.

TO SERVE
vegetable or cottonseed oil, for deep-frying
sifted confectioners' sugar, for dusting

Use an ice cream scoop to scoop out two or three balls of the cheesecake per serving, then roll into balls the size of golf balls. Chill in the freezer for 30 minutes prior to frying.

When you're ready to serve and assemble, heat about 4 inches (10 cm) of vegetable oil in a deep fryer or large heavy-based saucepan to 325°F (170°C), or until a cube of bread dropped into the oil turns golden brown in 20 seconds.

Working in batches, drop the cheesecake balls into the batter and coat them thoroughly. Give them a quick shake to flick off some of the excess batter. (The excess deep-fried batter is delicious, by the way!)

Immediately add the cheesecake balls to the hot oil and cook for about 5 minutes, or until golden. Drain briefly on a paper towel, dust with confectioners' sugar, and prepare to quickly assemble your desserts.

TO ASSEMBLE
Smear the passion fruit curd around each serving bowl, then some of the salted caramel.

In each bowl, build a stack of deep-fried cheesecake balls, cheesecake ice cream, and caramel popcorn.

Drizzle with the remaining salted caramel and serve immediately.

MILKSHAKES

The beauty of milkshakes is that you can customize them as much or as little as you please using different ice creams, spices, jams, fruit purées, toppings, and spreads. We also make adults-only versions of our shakes by adding a nip of alcohol. Bourbon and spiced rum go particularly well with the Classic Vanilla Shake. [Each milkshake serves 1]

CLASSIC VANILLA MILKSHAKE

1 scoop vanilla ice cream
¼ teaspoon vanilla bean paste
1 tablespoon malted milk powder
1 cup (8 fl oz/250 ml) milk

Add all the ingredients to a blender and blitz together until well combined. Using a handheld stick blender would work just fine, too!

CHOCOLATE MILKSHAKE

¼ cup (2 oz/55 g) sugar
¼ cup (1 oz/30 g) unsweetened cocoa powder
¼ cup (1½ fl oz/50 ml) heavy whipping cream (38% or more fat)
1 scoop chocolate ice cream
1 cup (8 fl oz/250 ml) milk

Put the sugar and ⅓ cup (2½ fl oz/80 ml) of water in a saucepan and boil until the sugar has dissolved. Turn off the heat, leaving the pan on the stove. Stir in the cocoa powder and whisk until dissolved. Turn the heat back to medium, add the cream and bring to a boil, then simmer, stirring frequently, for 10–12 minutes, or until thickened to a sauce.

Cool the pan in an ice bath; your chocolate sauce will keep in an airtight container in the fridge for up to 1 week.

When ready to serve, pour all your yummy chocolate sauce into a blender. Add the ice cream and milk and blitz together.

SALTED CARAMEL MILKSHAKE

9 oz (250 g) sweetened condensed milk, or a good splash of store-bought caramel sauce
1 teaspoon salt flakes
1 scoop vanilla ice cream
1 cup (8 fl oz/250 ml) milk

Make your own hands-free caramel by placing the unopened can of sweetened condensed milk in a saucepan of boiling water, making sure it is fully submerged. Simmer for 3 hours, topping up the water if needed. Let the can cool before removing from the water. Inside you'll find enough rich, gooey caramel for 5 milkshakes; your caramel will keep in an airtight container in the fridge for up to 1 week.

Add a good splodge of caramel to a blender. Add the remaining ingredients and blitz together until well combined.

PB&J MILKSHAKE

2 teaspoons blackberry jam
1 scoop vanilla ice cream
1 tablespoon smooth peanut butter
1 cup (8 fl oz/250 ml) milk

Drizzle the jam around the inside of your glass. Put the remaining ingredients in a blender, blitz together, then pour into your jam-lined glass.

GLOSSARY

ANGOSTURA BITTERS

A botanically infused liquid used for flavoring beverages, and occasionally food. Made by the House of Angostura in Trinidad and Tobago, it is more concentrated than other bitters. You'll find it in most good liquor stores.

APEROL

An Italian aperitif (a drink taken before a meal to stimulate the appetite). The recipe is unchanged since its creation shortly after World War I. It is bright orange in color and has a bittersweet taste. Kind of like how we feel pre-service.

APPLEJACK

Historically, applejack was an American spirit made by concentrating apple cider, either by freeze or evaporative distillation. These days it is a blend of apple brandy and neutral spirits. If you have trouble locating it in stores, you can find it online.

CHINESE RADISH

Also known as *daikon*, Chinese radish is a mild-flavored winter radish with a long, white root. It looks more like a fat, white carrot or cucumber than a regular radish.

CLAMATO

A mix of tomato juice concentrate, clam broth, and spices. It lifts a Caesar cocktail to a whole new level. Look for it in delicatessens.

CRÈME FRAÎCHE

Cream and buttermilk mixed together and left to thicken unrefrigerated for 12–24 hours, depending on conditions. You can put it on anything from muesli and fresh berries to hot soups to apple pie. You'll find it in the refrigerated section of large supermarkets.

CURING SALT

Used in food preservation to prevent or slow down spoilage. Particularly relevant for curing meats, it is a mix of table salt and sodium nitrate. It is sold in spice shops and specialty food stores.

ESPELETTE PEPPER

A variety of chili pepper that was originally cultivated in Espelette, a town in southwest France. Of mild heat, it can be used fresh, dried, ground, puréed, or pickled.

FRESNO CHILIES

Similar to a jalapeño pepper, the fresno chili can be used when it's green and in its infancy, adding a mild heat and flavor to anything from chutneys and dips to casseroles and stews. Red, mature chilies have less flavor but more heat, and are large enough to stuff with ingredients and cook on a barbecue.

JUMBO LUMP CRABMEAT

This just refers to the meat from fat crabs—specifically to the meat from the two muscles connected to the swimming legs. When a recipe calls for jumbo lump crabmeat, just get the fattest crabmeat you can find.

KEWPIE MAYONNAISE

A Japanese mayo made with rice vinegar, rather than the distilled vinegar used in traditional mayo. It's creamier and smoother than the regular stuff, and in our opinion, much better! You'll find it in large supermarkets and Asian food stores.

NIGELLA SEEDS

These little babies are often confused with fennel, cumin, onion, or caraway seeds. They aren't any of these, despite their oniony smell and slightly peppery flavor. Traditionally they're used in Indian and Middle Eastern cuisines.

OLD BAY SEASONING

An American herb and spice mix, primarily used in Southern cuisine. I've made my own when my shipment didn't arrive in time, using a mix of celery seeds, salt, red and black pepper, and paprika, and no one knew the difference. But I did. I think McCormick must put fairy dust in theirs—it's that good! Look for it in the spice aisle at the grocery store.

PERNOD

This unsweetened, aniseed-flavored liqueur has been helping people digest their meals since its inception in 1805.

PISCO

The debate as to whether this white brandy, made from Muscat grapes, originated in Peru or Chile is now over 400 years old. We're pretty happy to spend the next 400 years drinking pisco sours while they sort it out.

SHICHIMI TOGARASHI

A Japanese spice mix, usually containing chili, dried orange peel, sesame seeds, seaweed, and Sichuan peppercorns. It is used to season rice dishes, soups, noodles, and grilled meats, and is widely available from Asian supermarkets and good spice stores.

SMOKED SALT

This is salt that has been wood-smoked, imparting a very earthy, intense, aromatic flavor. If you can't do it yourself, buy it from spice shops, specialty food stores, or online.

SMOKED TOMATO PASSATA

Italian in origin, passata is like a tomato purée, sauce, or paste, only thicker. You wouldn't want to use anything else if this is called for in a recipe. We smoke ours because Gregory would smoke everything if he could.

TIKI BITTERS

An "island" bitters flavored by a blend of cinnamon, allspice, and a supporting cast of other spices. We use it in our pisco punch and iced teas. Probably best to track this one down online.

TUACA

A golden liqueur made from brandy, orange essence, and vanilla, with a faintly butterscotch flavor. The name comes from the two Italian families who originally produced it—Tuoni and Canepa.

WHITE BALSAMIC VINEGAR

Balsamic vinegar is made from the "must" (unfermented juice) of Trebbiano grapes. Unlike regular balsamic vinegar, which is dark in color, white balsamic vinegar has a golden hue, as the grapes are not allowed to caramelize during the simmering process.

WHITE SOY SAUCE

Light amber in color, and brewed with more wheat than soybeans, white soy sauce is fermented for a shorter time than regular soy sauce. It flavors foods and marinades without darkening them.

YUZU

A round, yellowish citrus fruit, originating in China and widely used in Korea and Japan.

RENDERING FAT

A few of the recipes in this book call for your favorite animal lard.
It's easy enough to make your own lovely lard at home, and in the case
of duck fat, it will save you a small fortune. Once strained, the rendered
fat will keep in an airtight container in the fridge for up to 2 months.
[Makes about 1 cup (8 oz/250 g)]

BACON FAT

1 lb 2 oz (500 g) flat belly bacon

Preheat the oven to 325°F (170°C). Put the
bacon in a roasting pan and roast for about
1 hour.

Transfer to a large stockpot and pour in
20 cups (175 fl oz/5 liters) of water. Bring to a
boil, then cook, uncovered, over medium–high
heat for about 30 minutes, until the water has
evaporated.

Turn the heat down to medium–low. Using
a metal spatula, scrape the fat off the bottom of
the pot, as it will want to stick; the fat will remain
a liquid throughout the cooking process.

Turn off the heat and leave the fat to cool for
about 15 minutes. Strain through a fine mesh
strainer to remove any impurities.

CHICKEN FAT

**1 lb 2 oz (500 g) chicken skin (ask your
butcher for this)**

Thoroughly rinse and dry the chicken skin,
then place in a large stockpot with 20 cups
(175 fl oz/5 liters) of water. Bring to a boil
over medium–high heat, then cook, uncovered,
for about 30 minutes, or until the water has
evaporated. The water will break down the skin;
the fat will come out of the skin and rise to the
surface; the skin will start to brown.

When all the water has evaporated, turn
the heat down to medium–low. Using a metal
spatula, scrape the skin off the bottom of the
pot, as it will want to stick. Continue to render
the skin in its own fat until it becomes golden
brown delicious; the fat will remain a liquid
throughout the cooking process.

Drain the skin on a paper towel; it will
become crispier as it cools.

Turn off the heat and leave the fat to cool for
about 15 minutes. Strain through a fine mesh
strainer to remove any remaining skin.

DUCK FAT

See the Duck's Nuts recipe on page 62.

PORK FAT

2 lb 4 oz (1 kg) pork back fat, diced

Preheat the oven to 325°F (170°C). Put the pork fat in a roasting pan and roast for about 1 hour.

Transfer to a large stockpot and pour in 20 cups (175 fl oz/5 liters) of water. Bring to a boil, then cook, uncovered, over medium–high heat for about 30 minutes, until the water has evaporated.

Turn the heat down to medium–low. Using a metal spatula, scrape the fat off the bottom of the pot, as it will want to stick; the fat will remain a liquid throughout the cooking process.

Turn off the heat and leave the fat to cool for about 15 minutes. Strain through a fine mesh strainer to remove any impurities.

LAMB FAT

2 lb 4 oz (1 kg) lamb belly

Preheat the oven to 325°F (170°C). Put the lamb in a roasting pan and roast for about 1 hour.

Transfer to a large stockpot and pour in 16 cups (140 fl oz/4 liters) of water. Bring to a boil, then cook, uncovered, over medium–high heat for about 30 minutes, until the water has evaporated.

Turn the heat down to medium–low. Using a metal spatula, scrape the fat off the bottom of the pot, as it will want to stick; the fat will remain a liquid throughout the cooking process.

Turn off the heat and leave the fat to cool for about 15 minutes. Strain through a fine mesh strainer to remove any impurities.

INDEX

PAGE NUMBERS IN ITALICS REFER TO PHOTOGRAPHS

THANK YOU!

In alphabetical order...

Amy Bayliss: For extricating the recipes out of Gregory's brain and into this book. And for her spreadsheets. And attention to detail.

Andy Bowdy: For his contributions to this book, but mostly for being one of Gregory's best mates, for believing in him since before we opened, and for being the reason handbooks about appropriate workplace behavior were invented.

Jill Dupleix and Terry Durack: For brokering the original deal, and for not seeming so scary when they aren't reviewing you.

The Edie Elves: Alex, Gabs, Nadine, and particularly Naomi's parents, who donated a couple of days a week while Q was in daycare, enabling Naomi to be the only kind of working mum her heart could let her be. Naomi wrote in one room, they held Edie in the next.

Fellow Sydney chefs and restaurateurs: Thanks for opening your arms and welcoming us into the fold. Now if only we could all get some time off to actually hang out together...

Friends and extended family: We are surrounded by the most incredible people, and sharing in their interesting and clever lives nourishes us in return. The belief of those who matter allows you to do the damndest things.

Hart family: We know that every step we take, as parents and as business owners, can be chaperoned as much or as little as we require by various members of Team Hart. How very fortunate we are to belong.

Fiona and Phil Hart: Did we mention Naomi's parents already? That's okay, they deserve a second mention. We'll never be able to adequately express our gratitude or repay them for their unconditional love. Except to say that it is returned.

Hartsyard regulars: Some from our very first night of opening. Thank you most sincerely for your continued support. We've enjoyed getting to know you and hearing your stories. Thank you for becoming our friends.

Hartsyard team: What a loyal, skilled, fun group of people we employ, some of you since day one. Thank you for helping to create the extraordinary and complex dynamic we have at Hartsyard. We rely on you, joke with you, care about you, grow and learn from you, and are intensely grateful for your constant hard work and commitment.

John Laurie: For his inspired photography, his low-key style, and for "getting" Gregory within seconds of their first meeting.

Franny Llewellyn: For her endless supply of handmade napkins, for transcribing the family recipes, and for being our Old Bay smuggler.

The Llewellyns: Who temper Gregory's memories with reality and provide enthusiasm, love, and family recipes from afar.

Mads and Mark: Our fun and funny front of house managers. Loyal, lovely, and obliged us with the drinks recipes when we asked.

Karlene Meenahan and Paul Venables: For reading version two of Naomi's ramblings and for providing honest, loving, and thoughtful feedback.

Jane Morrow: Our publisher and, significantly for Naomi, a fellow working mum. At the end of every email, full of encouragement and clever ideas, and proof that this working–parenting malarkey might actually be achievable.

Phill Morgan: Neither Naomi nor Gregory had anything to do with the GBD ("golden brown delicious") name. All credit to Phill the chicken technician.

The Murdoch Books team: Virginia Birch, Hugh Ford, Sue Hines, Jane Morrow, and Katri Hilden—clever, creative, enthusiastic, and nurturing. We were truly delighted to be asked to do this project, and they all made it a wonderful, inclusive process.

Matt Page: For enhancing Gregory's creations, so John's photos could really rock.

Dave and Jennie Smiedt: Regulars since our first week, when Gregory made Jennie cry. Dave wrote the foreword for this book and sometimes drops off cologne to make Gregory smell better.

Thunder Bay Press
An imprint of Printers Row Publishing Group
10350 Barnes Canyon Road, Suite 100, San Diego, CA 92121
www.thunderbaybooks.com

First published in 2015 by Murdoch Books, an imprint of Allen & Unwin.
This edition published in 2016 by Thunder Bay Press

Murdoch Books Australia
83 Alexander Street
Crows Nest NSW 2065
Phone: +61 (0) 2 8425 0100
Fax: +61 (0) 2 9906 2218
murdochbooks.com.au
info@murdochbooks.com.au

Murdoch Books UK
Erico House, 6th Floor
93–99 Upper Richmond Road
Putney, London SW15 2TG
Phone: +44 (0) 20 8785 5995
murdochbooks.co.uk
info@murdochbooks.co.uk

Thunder Bay Press
Publisher: Peter Norton
Publishing Team: Lori Asbury, Ana Parker, Laura Vignale
Editorial Team: JoAnn Padgett, Melinda Allman, Traci Douglas

Library of Congress Cataloging-in-Publication Data
Llewellyn, Gregory, author.
  Fried chicken & friends / Gregory Llewellyn and Naomi Hart.
     pages cm
  Includes bibliographical references and index.
  ISBN 978-1-62686-588-4 (hardcover cloth : alk. paper)
1. Cooking, American--Southern style. I. Hart, Naomi, author. II. Title. III. Title: Fried chicken and friends.
  TX715.2.S68L66 2016
  641.5975--dc23

                                              2015030104

20 19 18 17 16   1 2 3 4 5

Printed in China

IMPORTANT: Those who might
be at risk from the effects of
salmonella poisoning (the elderly,
pregnant women, young children,
and those suffering from immune
deficiency diseases) should
consult their doctor with any
concerns about eating raw eggs.

OVEN GUIDE: You may find
cooking times vary depending
on the oven you are using. For
fan-forced ovens, as a general rule,
set the oven temperature to 35°F
(20°C) lower than indicated in the
recipe.

MEASURES GUIDE: We have used
20 ml (4 teaspoon) tablespoon
measures. If you are using a 15 ml
(3 teaspoon) tablespoon, add an
extra teaspoon of the ingredient
for each tablespoon specified.